Harry Kane: The Inspiring Story of One of Soccer's Star Strikers

An Unauthorized Biography

By: Clayton Geoffreys

Table of Contents

Foreword

Over the course of his career, Kane has established himself as one of the greatest strikers to ever play the game. Since going pro, Kane has accomplished a lot over the course of his career, playing the greater part of it for the Tottenham Hotspur. Renowned for his prolific goalscoring, Kane has scored over 350 goals for the Premier Clubs and the England national team. He surpassed Wayne Rooney and as of this writing, is the second-highest all-time goal scorer in the Premier League at 213. After his 19 years with the Tottenham Hotspur, Kane bid goodbye and moved to Bayern Munich in 2023. He signed up for a four-year contract worth 110 million euros, joining the list of Bundesliga's most expensive transfers in history. Thank you for purchasing *Harry Kane: The Inspiring Story of One of Soccer's Star Strikers*. In this unauthorized biography, we will learn Harry Kane's incredible life story and impact on the game of soccer. Hope you enjoy and if you do, please do not forget to leave a review!

Also, check out my website at claytongeoffreys.com to join my exclusive list where I let you know about my latest books. To thank you for your purchase, you can go to my site to download a free copy of *33 Life Lessons: Success Principles, Career*

Advice & Habits of Successful People. In the book, you'll learn from some of the greatest thought leaders of different industries on what it takes to become successful and how to live a great life.

Cheers,

Clayton Geoffreys

Visit me at www.claytongeoffreys.com

Introduction

Harry Edward Kane is one of the most recognizable faces in English and world football, owing to his potency in front of goal. Noted as one of the best contemporary forwards of his generation, Kane has made history with Tottenham Hotspur and the England national team. He became the all-time top scorer for his national team in 2023.[i]

Despite initially struggling to break into a Tottenham Hotspur setup, Kane played for various other clubs on loan while waiting for his opportunity to play for the Spur's first team. After this, he went on to become a club legend[ii] owing to his ability to inspire winning performances, especially against North London rivals, Arsenal.

Kane's prestige with the national team is not exclusively attributed to his goal tally for England but to his role as national team captain. He has been praised for his roles in both the 2018 World Cup and the 2022 European Championship in which the Three Lions reached the semi-final and final respectively. The latter saw England reach their first major international tournament final since 1966.

His services to football have transcended beyond the pitch, as he has received accolades from the British government and monarchy. He was awarded an MBE[iii] and the Freedom of the City.[iv] These accompany a whole host of other individual awards that Kane has acquired throughout his career, including World Cup top scorer, and Premier League Golden Boot. However, Kane has a distinct lack of trophies. Despite being one of the top strikers in the Premier League for the best part of a decade, Tottenham has failed to win a single competitive trophy[v] leaving Kane without any kind of winner's medal.

Chapter 1: Childhood and Early Life

Harry Kane was born on July 28, 1993. His parents are Patrick and Kim Kane, and he has an older brother named Charlie. His father Patrick is of Irish ancestry, giving Kane some connection to the Emerald Isle, and his mother Kim was born and raised in London. Kane identifies as a Londoner having been born in Walthamstow.

Harry's football roots run deep, particularly on his mother's side. Harry's maternal grandfather, Eric Hogg, was an accomplished footballer himself. He played at a semi-pro level for the Blundell Rovers in the 1960s, and then later for Brentwood and Warley. Eric had five brothers who also played, and the Hogg boys loved the sport so much that they even formed their own youth team in Islington in the 1940s. (Incidentally, the eldest Hogg boy was also named Harry.)

Harry attended Larkswood Primary Academy and the Chingford Foundation School,[vi] where he played football on the concrete pitches during his lunchtime breaks. It was there that he was inspired to play football, as the school was famous for David Beckham having previously studied there too.

In football terms, there is much conjecture about which London club Harry supported. Of course, the obvious answer would be that he supported Tottenham Hotspur.[vii] However, during his rise at Spurs, multiple photographs emerged online of him wearing Arsenal shirts as a young boy,[viii] and that included images of him with his hair dyed red on a trophy parade for the Arsenal Invincibles. Kane has seldom commented on that viral content but when asked, he's been quick to dismiss being called an Arsenal fan, saying that he was simply part of the Arsenal academy[ix] at the time.

Chapter 2: Youth Career

It didn't take long for Harry Kane to get involved with football as he joined a local club, the Ridgeway Rovers,[x] at the age of six. David Beckham had previously played at this club as a youngster, so Kane was clearly on a similar career trajectory! Beckham and Kane had also famously been photographed together during Kane's time there as a boy.

After two years with Ridgeway Rovers, Harry was spotted by the scouting team from Arsenal. As a result, in 2001, he joined the Arsenal academy[xi] as an eight-year-old. However, after a few seasons of tracking his progress, the Arsenal youth staff decided that at the age of 12, it was time to release the youngster, believing that he would not be able to reach the desired level for the club.

When the Arsenal staff decided that Benik Afobe would be a better fit[xi] for the Arsenal future, Kane briefly returned to the Ridgeway Rovers before having a trial at Watford.[xii] It was during his short stint with the Hornets that he was noticed by Tottenham Hotspur[xiii] (in a match he played against Spurs) and was invited to join the club's academy project.

Since then, Harry worked his way up the rankings at Tottenham Hotspur through the various youth and reserve teams. Notably, in his last full season in the U18 side, he played 22 times and scored 18 goals[xiv] until he was called upon by the first team in the 2009-10 season.

Chapter 3: Professional Club Career

2009-10: Spotted on the Tottenham Bench

The first time that Harry Kane was involved with any kind of Tottenham Hotspur first team was in 2009 when the fresh-faced striker was named on the bench by Harry Redknapp for a League Cup (the competition Tottenham had won the season before)[xv] fixture against Everton. The Spurs won the match 2-0[xvi] and progressed to the next round, however, Kane neither came off the bench in this match, nor was he named in any further squad in the competition.

Redknapp would name Kane on the bench one further time throughout the season, as the young striker was on the sidelines for a FA Cup fifth-round replay against Bolton Wanderers at White Hart Lane. Yet Kane was not needed on the night, as Tottenham triumphed 4-0[xvii] and progressed to the next phase.

Harry would not be seen again for the remainder of the season. Tottenham did not win either competition that season as a barren trophy run started for the beleaguered club.

2010-11: Loan Spell with Leyton Orient in League One

Despite Redknapp placing Kane on the bench twice in the 2009-10 season, he did not afford the young striker the same opportunity in the proceeding campaign. Kane disappeared from the first-team subs contention.

After half a season of inactivity, it was announced in January 2011 that Kane would join Leyton Orient in League One for the remainder of the season.[xviii] At the time, the O's were eyeing the chance of promotion to the EFL Championship. Harry would come off the bench just four days after moving to the team, making his professional football debut as a substitute in a 1-1[xix] draw away at Rochdale.

Kane would score in his first home match in front of his supporters at Brisbane Road, as Leyton Orient went on to defeat Sheffield Wednesday 4-0.[xx] Harry would continue to be in and out of the O's squad as the team jostled for playoff contention. His next major contribution would be an iconic substitute appearance when he scored two goals in the last twenty minutes in a 4-1 win[xxi] against the Bristol Rovers.

After that game, Kane scored a further two goals for the club but ultimately could not help the team reach the playoffs.

Agonizingly, Leyton Orient finished just one point off AFC Bournemouth, who sealed the last qualification berth. In total, Kane scored five goals in 25 appearances (mostly subbed on or off).

Even after leaving the club, Kane remained amicable with the board, having continued to work with Leyton Orient despite his fame reaching superstardom and the club facing multiple relegations in the seasons long after Kane's departure. This includes fronting money to sponsor the club and donating the shirt space to a mental health charity.[xxii]

2011-12: Helping Spurs in UEFA Europa League

Tottenham Hotspur qualified for the UEFA Europa League through a fifth-place finish in the Premier League season in the 2010-11 campaign. Even with a stacked attacking roster that included Emmanuel Adebayor, Louis Saha, Giovani dos Santos and Jermain Defoe, the manager, Harry Redknapp, still saw a spot for Kane in the squad. This was to be a rotation option in the UEFA Europa League.

The Spurs had to first navigate a playoff-round tie against Heart of Midlothian FC before taking their place in the group stage.

Redknapp's team won the first match in Scotland[xxiii] with relative ease, and they took a 5-0 advantage back to London.

Given the colossal score line and the gulf in quality between the sides, Redknapp decided to field a very youthful-looking eleven for the reverse fixture at White Hart Lane. This would be Harry Kane's professional debut for Tottenham Hotspur.[xxiv] Harry would notably win a penalty for the team and have it saved[xxv] as the game ended 0-0.

Having qualified for the group stage, Kane was yet to be named among the squad for Tottenham's UEFA Europa League games as the 18-year-old tried to etch a name for himself in the famous white shirt. While he had little impact on the first five games (of six), he scored his first-ever Tottenham Hotspur goal in the final group stage match against Shamrock Rovers[xxvi] at Tallaght Stadium in Dublin, Ireland.

Despite the game ending 4-0 in favor of the Spurs, other results and prior games meant that Tottenham would only finish third in their group and would not continue their continental expedition.[xxvii] With that competition finished for Spurs, Redknapp felt that he could not play the youngster in the Premier League so he instead put him on the loan list for the upcoming winter transfer window.

2011-12: January Loan Transfer to Millwall

Needing game time for his development and facing a lack of opportunities in the Tottenham first team, Harry completed a January loan move to Millwall FC.[xxviii] Upon joining the Lions at the Den, Millwall was a club in dire straits. Staring relegation down the barrel, Kane was thrust straight into the starting eleven.

Kane made his debut in a losing 1-0 effort to Bristol City,[xxix] as the loanee had a shot comfortably saved by veteran and former England keeper, David James. His second game would be a lot more memorable—but for the wrong reasons. Harry Kane and Millwall endured a horrific 6-0 loss at home to Birmingham City[xxx] as the situation at the London club became very apparent. In short, the club needed a tremendous amount of help to get better. Luckily, they now had a player who would soon become a tremendous striker amongst their ranks, even if they didn't know it yet!

It took a while for Kane to make a tangible difference to Millwall's form, but eventually, it came. The club also stuck by their manager, Kenny Jackett, which helped Kane keep some consistency in the system. Kane ended up scoring his first goal for the Lions in a 3-1 victory at Turf Moor against Burnley in late February. The future England captain looked energized throughout the entirety of this match[xxxi] as the loan move looked like it would finally bear fruit.

The results would remain inconsistent for Millwall, but the signs were there that Harry Kane could be a pivotal player for the team. His next goal came in the away game at Peterborough with a superb long-range effort as Millwall won 3-0[xxxii] and took a big step toward staying in the Championship.

After two subsequent losses to Nottingham Forest and Southampton, Kane was again on the scoresheet as he scored in the 3-0 triumph against the Doncaster Rovers. As the Rovers were at the bottom of the table, this result vindicated the notion that Millwall had enough quality to avoid the drop.

However, come April 2012, both the club and Kane entered a purple patch of form. Millwall went unbeaten in its last six games, winning five of them as Kane scored four goals in the process. The result saw Millwall reach 16th position in the table, multiple spots above the relegation zone. Kane ended the season having scored seven goals in the Championship and another two in the FA Cup. Overall, he made 27 appearances for the club during his loan.

Upon reflection on his loan at Millwall, Kane spoke highly of his experience at the club:

"My loan at Millwall was a big part of my development. I was 18, we were in a relegation battle, and it turned me into a man. I played in difficult, high-pressure games and I managed to come out of it positively."[xxxiii]

Harry returned to Tottenham after the football league season. He was named on the Premier League bench for the Spurs' last game of the season when they defeated Fulham 2-0, although he did not participate in the match.

2012-13: Loan to Norwich City, Injured Tenure

Tottenham Hotspur was under new management for the 2012-13 season as the team hired the former Chelsea boss, Andre Villas-Boas. Ultimately, Harry Kane was not part of the new coach's plans. The Englishman came off the bench for the final five minutes of the opening games of the season but was dropped by the second match.

This prompted another loan move for Harry as he joined fellow Premier League side Norwich City.[xxxiv] He came off the bench in a home game against West Ham United for his Norwich debut. Despite capitalizing on a mistake by Robert Snodgrass to play him through on goal, Kane was unable to make any difference to the score line as it ended 0-0.[xxxv]

That 19-minute appearance would be one of his few outings for Norwich, as Kane was soon sidelined by a metatarsal fracture[xxxvi] which would keep him out for around three months.

Kane returned to the squad in late December 2012 as the team lost consecutive games to both Manchester City and West Ham United. The move was then curtailed early by Tottenham,[xxxvii] as they believed the young player was not getting enough game time. Therefore, Harry left the Canaries after just five appearances for the team. He scored no goals for the first team, and this loan move is regarded as one of Kane's most challenging and unproductive spells[xxxviii] during his career.

2012-13: Changing Lanes with Leicester City

Despite recalling Kane, the idea was not to play him in the first team with the Lilywhites; the upper management wanted to redeploy him someplace where would be played. That was when Leicester City in the Championship answered the call and agreed to take the forward player on a short-loan[xxxix] deal to help with their bid for promotion to the top flight of English football.

19

Much like his last loan in the second tier, Kane was put into the starting eleven immediately upon his arrival. While his debut for Leicester yielded a 0-0 result, his second was much better. His efforts inspired a 3-0 win against Blackburn Rovers,[xl] getting on the score sheet in the process. If Kane could be the same incarnation of himself that played so well for Millwall at this level, then Leicester could dream big of getting promoted.

But sadly, the goals dried up for Kane and the results for the team slipped as well. While the team climbed as high as the third spot during Kane's tenure at the club, poor results saw them drop to sixth in the league after the campaign.

Kane was brought on for both of the playoff games against Watford, yet he failed to make a difference. Leicester would lose the tie 3-2 on aggregate.[xli]

In addition to making these appearances for the Foxes, the club also holds a piece of Harry Kane history. As of the 2022/23 season, Kane has scored the highest number of goals against this team, having netted 20 times[xlii] against his former club.

2013-14: Eventual Spurs Breakthrough

Before the start of the season, Kane was placed in a few of the pre-season friendlies for Tottenham. He notably scored in the friendly against Monaco.[xliii] However, his general performance and prior outings for England in the U20 World Cup attracted lots of criticism.

"This is appalling. Suddenly Harry Kane is clean through on goal but he overruns the ball with an appalling touch, allowing Subasic to smother it. He's supposed to be a professional footballer … Really, though, what is Harry Kane doing in Tottenham's squad?"[xliv]

Back at Spurs, Andre Villas-Boas was entrusted to start the 2013-14 season, having secured the UEFA Europa League participation from the prior campaign. Owing to a lack of attacking players, (unlike prior years) Tottenham again saw the need to keep Harry Kane around to bolster their ranks, especially during the tricky European away days, as well as topping the numbers up.

As such, Kane played a bit part in Tottenham's two-legged qualification for the UEFA Europa League as he played against Dinamo Tbilisi from Georgia. Spurs won 8-0 on aggregate,[xlv] but Kane did not score. Harry would then have to wait an extended period because Villas-Boas still did not like what he saw from the Englishman. One cameo, an eight-minute appearance in the Premier League against Cardiff City, and 21 minutes in the Europa League opposing FC Sheriff was the totality of his game time for quite a while as he was mostly forced to sit on the bench.

However, Kane did play in two of Tottenham's games in the League Cup, notably finding the net against Hull City[xlvi] with a goal that would take the game to a penalty shoot-out. Kane would also convert his penalty successfully and the Spurs would proceed in this cup competition.[xlvii]

However, even sitting on the bench soon became impossible for Harry Kane, as a back injury would rule him out in November and give him niggling problems until February 2014. During that time, Daniel Levy, the Spurs' owner, ran out of patience with Andre Villas-Boas after poor results. This ushered in Tim Sherwood[xlviii], a former Tottenham player who wanted to step into management and help the team he had previously played for.

This period was instrumental to Kane's exposure to first-team top-level football, as it was the first time he was consistently trusted by a manager to play for Tottenham. Tim Sherwood has long since claimed responsibility for Kane's ascendency and explained that he had to fight to keep him when he arrived at the club in December 2013:

"Truth be known, if Tottenham had had their way ... then Harry Kane would not have been Harry Kane today, because he would have been on loan at a Championship club to gain even more experience. And he would not have got his opportunity to play for Tottenham."[xlix]

As he managed to keep Kane on the books at Tottenham during the winter window, Harry's name started to crop up on the bench again at the start of 2014. After a dismal showing at Anfield where Liverpool defeated Tottenham 4-0, Sherwood turned to youth and sparked Kane's career amid speculation that he would be dismissed.

Sherwood gave Harry Kane his Premier League debut at the age of 20 when he turned to the young striker for their game against Sunderland AFC. The change in personnel rejuvenated Tottenham as they brushed off some wretched form to win 5-1 with Kane scoring and assisting[l] on his first Premier League start for the club.

This led Harry to go on a small run of form as he scored in the next two Premier League games, as Tottenham drew with West Bromwich Albion[li] and defeated Fulham.[lii] Tottenham fans started to take notice of this youngster who had scored in three consecutive games for the club.

The team was still competing in the UEFA Europa League at this time, having qualified from the group stage. Kane played a culminating seven minutes in the two legs against FC Dnipro and the Spurs won 3-2 on aggregate.[liii] Kane would play a larger part in the team's Round of 16 tie against Benfica.

After a 3-1 loss in London, the Spurs went to Portugal needing a miracle—and almost got one. Kane was brought on for the final 20 minutes and turned the game on its head with two critical assists for Nacer Chadli[liv] within 60 seconds of each other. But it was not meant to be, as a late penalty call for Spurs wasn't given and Benfica scored an injury-time goal to give them a 5-3 aggregate victory.[lv]

Tottenham would end up finishing sixth in the league, but the emergence of a new star would keep Tim Sherwood in the role of Tottenham boss over the summer.

2014-15: Still Vying for Spurs Starting Spot

Despite his fantastic performances toward the end of the 2013-14 season, Harry Kane still found himself on the fringes come the start of the 2014-15 campaign. This was largely because he had to again prove himself when Tim Sherwood departed the club. Daniel Levy decided to appoint former Southampton boss Mauricio Pochettino[lvi] as his successor.

Kane was part of the team that traveled to the United States pre-season tour, and he scored the opening goal in their last match of the summer project. This set up a 2-0 win against Chicago Fire.[lvii]

Kane would also open the scoring in their next friendly. Tottenham defeated Celtic in Helsinki, Finland,[lviii] by a thumping 6-1 score, and this would set Kane and the entire team in good position as they were ready for the new season.

That said, it did not take long for him to make a difference for Tottenham in competitive action when he was afforded the chance. In the opening game of the season, Kane was brought on for the last few minutes, in which he set up Eric Dier for the winning goal[lix] against West Ham United.

While Kane jostled with the other attacking players for a starting position in the Premier League, he was afforded lots of time in the UEFA Europa League, a competition that Spurs were becoming synonymous with. Firstly, the team needed to navigate the playoff tie with AEL Limassol, a team from Cyprus. Kane scored in both the away and home legs[lx] and Spurs emerged as 5-1 aggregate winners.

Mauricio Pochettino wanted to create two distinct squads for the early part of the season in which the team had to compete in the

Premier League and the other cup competitions. Kane was part of the latter and rose to the challenge. Kane scored in Tottenham's first three league cup games as they brushed past Nottingham Forest, Brighton & Hove Albion, and Newcastle United.

On the continent, Kane also proved to be more than a handful for opposing defenders. This included a goal against Besiktas in a 1-1 draw as well as Kane's first-ever career hat-trick, as he netted three against Asteras Tripolis.[lxi] That 5-1 win was a remarkable match for Kane as he quickly stepped into goal when Hugo Lloris was sent off.[lxii] Unsurprisingly, he did not look convincing between the sticks and let in a free-kick effort after fumbling the ball.

Back out on the pitch as a striker, he followed that up with another goal against the Greek opposition away from home when the Spurs cruised to the knockout phase, despite finishing second in the group[lxiii] behind Besiktas.

Come the start of November 2014, Pochettino started to indulge supporters with what they wanted. Harry Kane starting games in the Premier League. After scoring a last-minute winner via a free kick at Villa Park,[lxiv] it was clear that Kane could make a difference at the top level. As Tottenham entered this game in the lowly position of eighth (compared to expectations), it has been said that Kane's last-gasp goal saved Pochettino from being fired[lxv] as Tottenham boss. As such, Kane was removed from the fringes of the team and thrust into the starting eleven plans.

This began with a goal against Hull City in the Premier League before he starred in a series of wins for the club in a winter period during which he came to life, notably scoring in three consecutive games against Swansea City, Burnley, and Leicester City. In each of those matches, Tottenham won 2-1. The latter of which took place on Boxing Day 2014[lxvi] as Kane closed out the year in fine fettle.

Harry Kane saw 2015 as an opportunity to finally make his mark, and he got started with an inspired performance for Tottenham on New Year's Day. This led to a 5-3 win against Chelsea[lxvii] in which he scored twice and set up two other goals. Given that the Spurs had not defeated Chelsea at White Hart Lane in almost five years, Kane's stature at the club was now reaching iconic status. Clearly, he was integral to the club re-finding its groove.

Kane continued this form as he scored twice against West Bromwich Albion[lxviii] in a 3-0 win. The next match would be

Kane's debut in the North London Derby as Tottenham played Arsenal. After going down a goal from Mesut Ozil, Kane battled on to be the difference in the match, bagging another brace[lxix] to give all three points to Tottenham. After scoring the winning goals in his first NLD, Kane commented:

"It's up there with my best feelings ever. The fans were incredible the whole game, the atmosphere was probably the best I've ever heard it (at White Hart Lane) and to be able to repay them with three points in the north London Derby is a moment everyone will remember."[lxx]

This iconic performance was followed up by goals against Liverpool and West Ham, and Harry Kane quickly became one of the standout stars in the Premier League. His goals were again the difference between winning and losing for Tottenham when he scored both Spurs' goals in a 2-1 win against Queens Park Rangers.[lxxi]

Back on the continent, Tottenham was drawn against Fiorentina. Now established in the Premier League, Kane was used sparingly in both the home and away legs. He could not make a difference in either match as he played around 50 minutes across them both. Subsequently, Tottenham crashed out of the competition through a 3-1 aggregate[lxxii] win for the Italians in the Round of 32 phase.

Kane then notched up his first-ever Premier League hat trick as he bustled the net three times against his former club, Leicester City,[lxxiii] in a game that ended 4-3 to the Spurs. His next game in the competition was also remarkable as he took the captain's armband for the first time.[lxxiv] This was due to key senior team members Hugo Lloris, Younes Kaboul, and Jan Vertonghen all missing from the squad. However, the game itself against Burnley was a drab affair as it finished 0-0. Kane would also wear the armband in the proceeding match against Aston Villa.

Harry scored two more goals for Tottenham in league competition, with the team placing fifth in the league. Kane finished with 21 goals in 34 Premier League appearances, just 5 goals fewer than the eventual Golden Boot winner, Sergio Aguero.

In the two domestic cup competitions, Tottenham were knocked out of the FA Cup by Leicester City,[lxxv] however, Kane seldom featured in the competition. Nevertheless, the League Cup was a huge success for the team, having made it to the semi-finals in 2014. Now in the new year, Tottenham faced Sheffield United, who were playing in League One at the time. Kane proved to be the key difference, as the tie was in the balance in the final few minutes. Harry's sublime pass allowed Christian Eriksen to level up the match result on the night at 2-2,[lxxvi] silencing Bramall Lane and ensuring that Tottenham would qualify for the final 3-2 on aggregate.

This would be Tottenham's first appearance in the League Cup final since 2009 when they lost to Manchester United on penalties,[lxxvii] but Harry Kane was not selected for the matchday squad in that game. Spurs' supporters were hoping to replicate the feeling from the 2008 final when they defeated Chelsea 2-1[lxxviii] to lift the trophy. However, this final in 2015 proved to be more difficult for Tottenham when Chelsea exacted revenge on the day by taking the cup back to Stamford Bridge[lxxix] and marking the first of Harry Kane's major runners-up medals with Spurs.

Kane did pick up an individual award, however, as he was named the PFA Young Player of the Year in 2015.[lxxx] He was also named in the PFA's Team of the Year[lxxxi] as well.

Despite the season concluding, there was still work for Tottenham Hotspur as the team was ushered off for two post-season friendlies. Kane scored both goals in the contest against the Malaysian League XI team[lxxxii] and Tottenham won the match 2-1. Then the team went to Sydney, Australia, where

Kane was again the difference, with his goal proving to be the winner against Sydney FC.[1]

2015-16: Playing 38 Games in Title Challenge

While Kane had become a first-team member in the last campaign, it was the 2015-16 season that saw him truly take the mantle as he would go on to play in every single match of the Premier League campaign.

In the pre-season, Tottenham went to the U.S., where they played as the opposition to the MLS All-Star team. Harry Kane got Spurs on the score sheet as he celebrated a goal[lxxxiii] in this marquee fixture, but it was the All-Star team that got the win at Dick's Sporting Goods Park. Kane did not score in any other friendly even though Tottenham played two further games in Munich as part of the 2015 Audi Cup.

Mauricio Pochettino was still entrusted with the role of the head coach of Tottenham Hotspur. He went on the offensive in the transfer market as he signed key players like Son Heung-min,[lxxxiv] Toby Alderweireld, and Kieran Trippier.

The arrival of the South Korean signaled the start of a fantastic working relationship. Kane and Heung-min would play 298 games together at Tottenham (as of the end of the 2022-23 season). This partnership has been pivotal[lxxxv] in both Kane's and Tottenham's development, as the two players have combined 60 times to create or score goals.

Tottenham Hotspurs' season started with a trip to Old Trafford, where they lost 1-0. The start of the season was by all accounts rather slow for both Kane and the club. It took over a month to register their first win in the Premier League.

Again, playing in the UEFA Europa League, the team enjoyed more success on the continent and for once did not have to play in a preliminary round. They were automatically placed in Group J alongside Qarabag FK, AS Monaco, and RSC Anderlecht. Kane scored in the victories against the Belgian team[lxxxvi] as well as the game contested in Azerbaijan.[lxxxvii] In addition to Spurs' 4-1 triumph over Monaco, the North London team breezed through their group as the winners[lxxxviii] to ensure they would play in the knockout phase again.

Kane scored his first Premier League goal of the season against Manchester City[lxxxix] as Tottenham tore apart the former champions with a 4-1 victory. Shortly after that, both the player and club would enter a very rich vein of form. Kane scored seven goals in four games, including a hat-trick against AFC

Bournemouth,[xc] a brace in the game with West Ham, and one in the North London derby.

Tottenham would lose another contest with Arsenal in the opening round of the League Cup. Mathieu Flamini scored twice in a 2-1 victory for Arsenal,[xci] which inflicted Kane's first loss in the rivalry game.

Positive results allowed Tottenham to steadily climb the Premier League table and gaze at potentially qualifying for the UEFA Champions League, instead of the Europa League. These ambitions became tangible targets with three consecutive wins to end the calendar year. Kane played a key role in the victories against Southampton, Norwich City, and Watford.

At this point, Leicester City were the surprise league leaders in the English top flight, having impressed under new boss Claudio Ranieri. Tottenham's January was consumed by a trilogy series of three matches with Leicester that would rock both clubs' respective seasons.

Firstly, the pair played at White Hart Lane in the third round of the FA Cup. Harry Kane stole the headlines[xcii] when his closing moments penalty secured a 2-2 draw and a replay match. That converted penalty would be a milestone for Kane because it was his 50th goal for Spurs[xciii] across all competitions.

The second installment in their series came in the Premier League as Leicester walked out of White Hart Lane with all three points after a slender 1-0 victory. Just 10 days after their first meeting in the FA Cup, the teams faced off at the King Power Stadium in Leicestershire.

Kane would only play 30 minutes in the match, but Tottenham would win[xciv] the game and advance to the next round, completing their exciting three-phase run of games. While Tottenham secured progression in the FA Cup, Leicester arguably claimed the greater prize by earning the win in the Premier League fixture.

The next tie in the FA Cup pitted Spurs against lower-league opposition as they traveled to the JobServe Community Stadium to play Colchester United. Kane again took the captain's armband for this match as he led the team to a 4-1 victory[xcv] to progress to the fifth round. Even with Kane leading the team again, this was not enough for Spurs to proceed any further, as Crystal Palace went to White Hart Lane and left with a 1-0 win,[xcvi] dumping Tottenham out of the FA Cup.

Back in the UEFA Europa League, Tottenham was once again tied against Fiorentina in the Round of 32 stage, and a small rivalry began to develop between the teams. Kane did not score in either leg but Spurs were able to win 4-1 on aggregate.[xcvii] Tottenham would lose both legs of the next round against Borussia Dortmund losing 5-1 on aggregate.[xcviii]

Harry remained determined to make a difference for Tottenham, as the UEFA Champions League qualification through the league standings still looked like an achievable target. Six consecutive Premier League victories hurtled Spurs into the title race with Leicester City. The Foxes had opened up the season run-in when they lost 2-1 at the Emirates[xcix] to Arsenal. Those three teams would now push each other as they all vied for the Premier League spoils.

The third and final North London derby of the season would be significant to the title race. If Kane could inspire a win against their bitter rivals, then Tottenham could top the table and pile on the pressure with Leicester watching on.

Kane scored an important goal to set up a winning position. Tottenham led 2-1 with 62 minutes on the clock, topping the Premier League table momentarily in the process. Yet, Arsenal would come back to draw the game 2-2.[c] Leicester went on to defeat Watford later in the day, amassing a five-point lead over the Spurs.

Harry Kane would do his best to keep up with the league leaders as he led the Spurs to Premier League wins against Aston Villa, AFC Bournemouth, and Liverpool. Despite picking up some momentum in the final few games of the season, including a 4-0 win away at Stoke City, where Kane scored twice,[ci] Tottenham would eventually falter.

First up, against West Brom where the team spurned the victory as they ended up drawing 1-1[cii]. However, the final nail in the Spurs' title ambitions came when the team threw away a 2-0 lead at Stamford Bridge. Leicester City had already earned a point the day before at Old Trafford,[ciii] meaning that Tottenham would need a win to stay in the title race. Kane scored to take the lead, but Chelsea came back to draw 2-2 in the end.[civ] Thus, Tottenham could no longer win the title and Leicester City was crowned champions.[cv]

Tottenham would go on to lose its two subsequent games in the Premier League and finish third place behind their fierce rivals, Arsenal, even though the latter had dropped out of the title race several weeks prior.

Regardless of the disappointment at losing out on the Premier League title, Kane still had a fantastic personal season in the division, scoring 25 goals. This ensured that he would win the Premier League Golden Boot for the first time[cvi] in his career.

2016-17: 29 Premier League Goals as Spurs Improve

Now three years into his Tottenham Hotspur project, Mauricio Pochettino was set to take the team back into the UEFA Champions League after an extended period of exclusively playing in the UEFA Europa League.

Harry Kane did not score in the club's pre-season friendly tour in Australia, but he did notch up two goals in their exhibition match against Inter Milan[cvii] in Oslo, Norway, in a game that would be an interesting warmup for their return to the UEFA Champions League.

Kane took the captain's armband for the second and third games of the Premier League season, as Spurs defeated Crystal Palace and drew 1-1 with Liverpool. However, it took until the senior members returned to the side for Kane to get scoring for Tottenham. He wrapped up the goals in a rout at Bet365 Stadium as Spurs defeated Stoke City 4-0[cviii] again.

In the UEFA Champions League, Tottenham was drawn against Bayer Leverkusen, CSKA Moscow, and AS Monaco. Kane would play in the first match, a losing effort to the French team.[cix] The game attracted a bumper crowd of over 85,000. Spurs were playing their European games[cx] at Wembley Stadium because they had officially decided to move out of White Hart Lane, although they still played their domestic games there for the season.

Harry continued to dominate when he scored the winner against Sunderland.[cxi] However, this game was marred by the sight of Kane coming off the field with an ankle injury.[cxii] This setback would take Kane out of action from late September until early November. He would miss five Premier League matches (Tottenham only won two without him), three UEFA Champions League group stage games, and their two games in the League Cup, which saw them exit when Liverpool easily defeated the team in Kane's absence.

Undeterred by his time out, Harry returned to the first-team lineup in the North London derby away at the Emirates. Despite the team going down on the scoreboard, Kane continued to press, scoring a pivotal goal to demonstrate that he had shaken off the ankle problems and allowing Tottenham to earn a point[cxiii] against their bitter rivals, Arsenal. Wanting to keep up his form in London derbies, Kane proved to be the stimulus in a key win against West Ham United; his goals turned the game on its head as Spurs came from behind to win 3-2.[cxiv]

Kane continued to score, even on the continent, as he stuck away a penalty against AS Monaco on the fifth matchday of the UCL competition. However, Spurs lost the game 2-1.[cxv] Because the team lost to the same opposition on the opening day and only picked up three points while Kane was injured between rounds two and four, Tottenham was knocked out of the UEFA Champions League.[cxvi]

The last game of the group stage would be against CSKA Moscow at Wembley Stadium, a standoff for the third-place position to see who would transfer to the UEFA Europa League and who would be out of European competition altogether. The Russian team might have taken the lead, but Tottenham would ultimately prevail as 3-1 winners,[cxvii] with Kane scoring the second on the night and subsequently qualifying for the UEFA Europa League.

Back in the Premier League, Kane scored his sixth and seventh goals of the season in a 5-0 victory over Swansea City[cxviii] as Tottenham romped the Welsh team at White Hart Lane. This large victory put the Spurs back in contention for a top-four spot after what had been an inconsistent season littered with too many stalemate results. Throughout late November and most of December, Kane struggled to score but the team results, for the most part, remained consistent.

Tottenham stormed to consecutive 4-1 triumphs against Southampton and Watford with Kane notching up three for himself in the process. In January, Tottenham opened the title race wide open with a 2-0 win against Chelsea.[cxix] This result saw Tottenham crawl into the top three and opened up the table for teams like Liverpool, Manchester City, and even Arsenal as all the teams now believed they could challenge for the Premier League title.

On the heels of a heroic team result, Kane wanted some personal glory in the next match, as he netted a marvelous hat-trick against West Bromwich Albion to send Tottenham second in the Premier League.[cxx] While Chelsea also won that weekend, there was a belief that, with enough luck, Tottenham could cut down their seven-point deficit and continue to challenge for the title.

Kane played no part in the team's first two FA Cup games as the team overcame both Aston Villa and Wycombe Wanderers. However, the England striker was called upon for the fifth-round tie at Craven Cottage against Fulham. Kane took the captain's armband and produced a captain's performance from the front as he scored all three goals[cxxi] in their epic 3-0 victory. The sixth round was against one of Kane's former teams, as he welcomed Millwall to White Hart Lane. However, Kane played just 10 minutes in the 6-0[cxxii] win.

February 2017 would be a defining period for Tottenham's season, and Harry Kane continued to showcase his elite skills at the highest level. However, even though they were the second-best team in the league at the time statistically, the Spurs remained very much behind Chelsea in the standings. Kane was again the difference between winning and losing when he netted the only goal in a game against Middlesbrough, two against Everton, and another hat-trick against Stoke City.

In the Europa League, Kane played in 180 minutes of their two-legged tie with Gent. The striker was unable to get on the scoresheet as Tottenham ended up losing 3-2 on aggregate,[cxxiii] thus seeing the team crash out of yet another cup.

Tottenham kept on winning in the Premier League. Of course, none of their prior wins that season could have tasted much sweeter than their final-ever match at White Hart Lane, as their historic old stadium opened up one last time on May 14, 2017, and the team played Manchester United. Kane scored to make it

2-0[cxxiv] and ensure that the Spurs' fans left the ground happy one final time. In the process, he scored the penultimate goal at the ground, but his then-England international teammate scored the last goal at the venue as Wayne Rooney pulled one back for Manchester United[cxxv] before time.

This result and others piled pressure on Chelsea to not drop points, but it was not enough, as they would win the title after a 1-0 victory against West Bromwich Albion,[cxxvi] and with two games to spare.

Despite losing the chance to win the Premier League, Harry put his goal-scoring antics into overdrive. Firstly, he scored four goals against Leicester City in a 6-1 win.[cxxvii] To this date, that remains his highest goal-scoring tally for a single match in club football.

Despite playing in the somewhat familiar surroundings of Wembley Stadium, Tottenham faltered in the FA Cup semi-final. Kane scored a goal, but Chelsea took the 4-2 victory[cxxviii] and progressed to the final.

On the final day of the 2016-17 season, Tottenham played Hull City. The game itself was merely an exhibition. Tottenham could not move up or down from second place in the standings, and Hull was already relegated, but a big moment in Harry

Kane's history emerged at the KCOM Stadium. Kane scored a hat-trick on the day while Tottenham emerged as 7-1 winners[cxxix] in East Yorkshire. This match still serves as Kane's biggest margin of victory in club league football.

With seven goals in his last two games of the campaign, Kane ensured that he had earned the Premier League Golden Boot for a second season running,[cxxx] having notched up 29. While the team finished second and qualified for the UEFA Champions League again, Tottenham fans ultimately reflected that, if Kane had not sustained that ankle injury, could the team have won more games and pushed Chelsea even further, or have won it themselves?

After the conclusion of the season, Tottenham played one post-campaign match against Kitchee SC in Hong Kong. Kane scored yet another goal,[cxxxi] and he continued to notch up goals across various locations on the globe.

2017-18: PL 100 Club Member, Progress in Europe

After White Hart Lane was closed at the end of the 2016-17 campaign, Tottenham needed an alternative venue to play their home games. With their new bespoke stadium not ready yet, it was announced that they would occupy Wembley Stadium[cxxxii] for the 2017-18 season. Kane adapted to life well at the club's temporary home by scoring there at the first time of asking, as he netted in a pre-season friendly against Juventus in a 2-0 victory.[cxxxiii]

Having been around the block for a while now as one of Tottenham's stars, noticeable trends emerged. One of which is that Harry always started the season slowly. In fact, he had never scored a Premier League goal for Tottenham in the month of August.[cxxxiv] While it seldom mattered, as he finished as the league's top scorer in the prior two seasons, it was still a notable distinction at the time. This trend continued in August 2017 as Tottenham won, lost, and drew without Kane scoring or assisting.

When he flipped over his calendar to September, however, Kane was a different man. Scoring in the first Premier League fixture of the month, he rattled Everton with a brace as Spurs won 3-0 at Goodison Park.[cxxxv] This form continued throughout the month as he went on to score two more braces in the victories over West Ham United and Huddersfield Town. The latter of which saw his manager publicly praise the striker after the 4-0 win:

"It's difficult to speak every three days about Harry Kane, to find the words to describe him ... He is fantastic. He is great in front of the goal and when we don't have the ball he is the first one available to run, to fight for the team. His mentality is fantastic, it makes him one of the best strikers in the world ... But Harry is still so young and the gap to improve is massive for him. That is our job: to try and push him to get better and better and better.[cxxxvi]

That September goal rush was not limited to the Premier League, however. In what could have been the team's biggest UEFA Champions League challenge yet, the London team was drawn against Real Madrid, Borussia Dortmund, and APOEL Nicosia. Kane lit up Wembley Stadium as he played a hand in all three (scoring two and assisting one) of Tottenham's goals in their 3-1 success[cxxxvii] against Dortmund on the opening match day.

Kane assisted in the landmark 3-1 victory against Real Madrid[cxxxviii] in London and then scored in the away win at Signal Iduna Park to defeat Dortmund 2-1.[cxxxix] The latter result ensured that Tottenham would finish as group winners, proving to critics that they did belong at this level.

Tottenham was equally impressive back in the Premier League when the team defeated Liverpool 4-1 at home[cxl] in a game that

Harry Kane commanded with two goals and an assist. However, the game also saw Kane suffer a hamstring injury.[cxli] Thus, Kane would miss the proceeding league match against Manchester United and the fourth round of the League Cup against West Ham. Spurs lost both without Kane on the pitch.

Luckily for Tottenham, Kane would be back from injury relatively soon. He returned to the fray in the following Premier League matchup against Crystal Palace. His involvement with the side again provided goals in the games against West Bromwich Albion and Leicester City, but Spurs endured a poor run as the team went on a winless streak in the league. Unsurprisingly, Harry was the man to break the bad spell when he scored twice in the 5-1 victory over Stoke City.[cxlii]

The next meaningful series of games for Kane came in late December when the team took on Burnley and Southampton. The Englishman scored consecutive hat-tricks[cxliii] in these matches, upping his tally for the season to 18 before January.

In the new year, Kane was again entrusted to make a difference in the club's FA Cup campaign. This included providing goals against AFC Wimbledon, Newport County, and Rochdale. The team made it to the sixth round of the competition with relative ease. However, Kane missed the latter tie against Swansea City when a minor ankle injury ruled him out of contention. Tottenham won without him and advanced to the semi-final.

From January 2018 to mid-April, Tottenham amassed an awe-inspiring, unbeaten run spanning 12 games in the Premier League. Kane's goals ensured that the team remained in the race for the top four spots, despite being several points behind the league leaders, Manchester City. This series saw Kane become a Premier League centurion as he scored his 100th goal in the competition in a 2-2 draw against Liverpool[cxliv] at Anfield.

After coming through a very tricky group in the UEFA Champions League, there was real optimism that Tottenham on their day could challenge any of Europe's elite. For the Round of 16, the team was drawn against Juventus. Having defeated the Italian team in pre-season, there was even more optimism that Kane could strike again to take Tottenham beyond this round. The forward would indeed score in the tie, with the first leg in Turin[cxlv] ending 2-2. It would be another exit, however, as the team lost 2-1 at Wembley,[cxlvi] handing Juventus a 4-3 aggregate win.

The FA Cup semi-final would yield yet more misery for Tottenham. While now playing all their home games at Wembley, Harry Kane and company could not make the most of the home advantage as Manchester United won 2-1,[cxlvii] again halting any trophy plans for the club.

Kane ended the season with another late goal flurry, notching up five in as many games to draw the curtain on the season. Tottenham finished third in the league, with Kane setting a new record high for goals as he got 30 for the season. However, unlike the prior two seasons, he was not awarded the Premier League Golden Boot because Mohamed Salah had scored two more.

2018-19: The Ligament Injury Season

With the construction of the new Tottenham Hotspur Stadium still not complete, the Spurs would continue to play at Wembley Stadium[cxlviii] for the foreseeable future. Kane went through the entirety of the pre-season without scoring for Tottenham, which was unusual for him because he had made it a habit to score in the past. But nevertheless, it did allow for the rare sighting of Tottenham Hotspur lifting a trophy as they won the pre-season tournament, the 2018 International Champions Cup,[cxlix] by defeating such teams as AS Roma and AC Milan.

Despite not scoring on the opening day of the Premier League season, Kane still ended his August goal drought[cl] with a goal against Fulham in a 3-1 win, and followed that up with another in a remarkable 3-0 away win at Old Trafford[cli] against Manchester United, still in the same month!

Mauricio Pochettino's team had been growing every year with consistent semi-final appearances and steady qualifications for the UEFA Champions League. However, the club's trophy cabinet was still pretty barren. The team struggled for consistency, having lost games against Liverpool and Watford after the initial wins.

Kane was not used in the early rounds of the League Cup as Pochettino shuffled his deck around for multiple competitions. He was, however, brought on in the quarter-final at the Emirates, and his assist was able to ensure a 2-0 victory[clii] for Tottenham and passage to the semi-final tie.

Spurs were dealt an ominous group in the UCL, much as they were the year prior. They sat alongside FC Barcelona, Inter Milan and PSV Eindhoven in Group B. Tottenham started the campaign in tragic form by losing to the Italian and Spanish teams. Kane would score in that losing effort to Barcelona and bag another three in the proceeding games against PSV.[cliii]

Despite taking the scenic route (winning just two games of the six played), Tottenham still somehow managed to qualify for the knockout phase by away head-to-head goals against Inter

Milan,[cliv] meaning that Christian Eriksen's strike at the San Siro on matchday one was of paramount importance.

Tottenham would continue to jostle for dominance with the other top clubs as Kane enjoyed great form between November and January 2019, identified by a multitude of goals. In the FA Cup, he came off the bench in the third-round match for the final 15 minutes and even scored. This led to a 7-0 win over Tranmere Rovers[clv] away from home. That game holds the distinction of being Harry Kane's largest-ever margin of victory in club football across all competitions. In the next round, however, Crystal Palace would knock them out 2-0.

In the middle of January, Kane suffered an ankle ligament injury[clvi] that would sideline him from the team. While Kane had scored the only goal in the first leg against Chelsea in the League Cup semi-final, he was nothing more than a spectator for the encounter at Stamford Bridge, as Chelsea would win on penalties and cut short another Tottenham trophy charge. Kane would also miss the home fixture against Borussia Dortmund in the Champions League Round of 16, yet Tottenham would go on to win that game 3-0,[clvii] even with Kane warming the bench.

Harry finally returned to the fray with a goal at Turf Moor against Burnley in the Premier League, although Tottenham would lose the game. Four more games passed and Kane remained in great form, but the team could not earn a win in the league.

Meanwhile, behind the scenes at the club, the upper management were finally ready to unveil their new stadium after having played at Wembley Stadium for an extended period by this point. On April 3, 2019, Tottenham Hotspur Stadium opened its doors for the very first time to Premier League football. Kane played the full 90 minutes against Crystal Palace but did not score, however, the fans were still pleased with a winning 2-0 result.

In the UEFA Champions League, however, Harry was on song in the concluding tie at Signal Iduna Park. He wrapped up the tie with the only goal in Germany[clviii] to see the North London team progress to the next round via a 4-0 aggregate win. The quarter-final matchup was against a familiar opponent, Manchester City, and Tottenham won the home tie 1-0.[clix] During the match, Kane sustained yet another injury to his ankle,[clx] the same one which had sidelined him earlier in the season.

It looked like Kane would not score or play another game in the Premier League when it became clear that the injury was relatively serious. However, Tottenham, even without their heroic player, was able to muster victories in the second leg against Manchester City[clxi] and then navigate the semi-final tie successfully against Ajax.[clxii] This meant that Tottenham Hotspur would compete in the UEFA Champions League final against Liverpool.

Perhaps owing to the time between the end of the domestic seasons and the showpiece of European football, Kane possibly had enough time to recover and play in the final—Tottenham's finest moment, reaching the pinnacle of club football with just one step to climb.

As it turned out, Kane was fit to start and played 90 minutes in the final. Yet, his involvement was not enough to keep out Liverpool, who scored in the first minute. The Reds ultimately took home the trophy[clxiii] to Liverpool.

Kane finished the season with 24 goals from his 40 appearances across all competitions. While the campaign resulted in a trip to the UEFA Champions League, it was another "what if" season, as Kane's chronic ankle injury undoubtedly cost the team goals, performances, and points throughout the year.

Harry has gone on record stating that this was one of the hardest moments in his career, and he finds it hard to watch the game back.[clxiv] He did state, however, that the experience would only motivate him in the future:

"I think it just motivates you to get better. With the Champions League final, you want to play in those games all the time. We know it's going to be tough to get back there this year and it's down to us to perform."[clxv]

2019-20: Change at Tottenham, Changing World

Now at their new home, the Tottenham Hotspur Stadium, Kane and the rest of the team wanted to push on and keep vying for glory. But despite coming close to silverware in multiple competitions, Kane still had not hoisted a major trophy other than last year's 2018 International Champions Cup in pre-season.

In the pursuit of pre-season trophies, Kane scored the only goal in Tottenham's opening Audi Cup game against Real Madrid[clxvi] when the team secured an early final appearance. Spurs would go on to collect the Audi Cup trophy, defeating Bayern Munich on penalties[clxvii] after a captivating 2-2 draw. Kane did not score in the match, but did score his spot-kick in the shootout.

After the frivolities of the summer, Tottenham commenced their season with an empathetic 3-1 victory over Aston Villa, with Kane scoring two on the day. However, the start of the season subsequently became riddled with inconsistencies, especially losing 7-2 at home to Bayern Munich in the UEFA Champions League.[clxviii] Kane continued to score, but the overall results led Daniel Levy to fire Mauricio Pochettino[clxix] from his role as Spurs boss in mid-November.

Kane explained that he enjoyed working under the exiting manager, saying, "Mauricio was an amazing manager for me... Great person. Great, great coach. Helped me a lot to get to where I am now. So I'm really appreciative of him."[clxx]

One day later, it was announced that the iconic Premier League manager, former Chelsea and Manchester United boss Jose Mourinho, was appointed as the head coach.[clxxi]

Life started well under Portuguese management. Kane scored in a 3-2 victory[clxxii] against West Ham in Mourinho's first match as Tottenham's manager. As Hugo Lloris was out of action for some time, Kane also enjoyed an extended period as the Spurs captain. This saw him take a critical role throughout November and December, including a stellar performance in a 5-0 victory against Burnley.[clxxiii]

However, come the start of 2020, Kane's season would be cast in doubt. The striker limped off in a 1-0 defeat to Southampton,[clxxiv] and it was later confirmed to be a serious long-term injury. Come March 2020, Kane still had not played and his injury persisted. Without him, Tottenham was knocked out of the UEFA Champions League and the FA Cup, and they dropped to eighth in the Premier League.

Kane's injury would not be the only factor in Tottenham's not winning in the proceeding months. At this time, the global COVID-19 pandemic had placed a hold on all football. The Premier League paused all operations and fixtures in March 2020 and no games took place until enough protocols were in place to play the games safely. Thus, games did not resume until June.[clxxv]

Despite Kane's initial injury assessment potentially ruling him out for the season, the enforced break actually allowed him to recover enough to play a part in Tottenham's campaign.[clxxvi] Harry was on the pitch in Spurs' first game back against Manchester United and would feature in all of their remaining games. However, it was the final run-in of three games in which Kane would score five goals.

While having Harry Kane back in the team was great for the team's goal tally, in the end, it could not salvage the season. Tottenham only finished sixth[clxxvii] in the league, qualifying for the UEFA Europa League, a far cry from the targets previously set. In an injury-plagued season also muddled with the disruption of COVID, Kane still scored 18 Premier League goals in 29 appearances.

2020-21: Empty Stadiums, Spurs Still Suffer

As the new season approached, the COVID-19 virus was still looming large and incredibly infectious. Thus, the Premier League, for the most part, played behind closed doors in the 2020-21 season—a real shame, given that Tottenham had only just opened its new state-of-the-art stadium.

Because the pandemic also restricted international travel, Tottenham, like most teams, played their pre-season games exclusively against domestic competition. However, Kane notably did not score in any of the four games that they participated in.

Kane started the 2020-21 season in turbulent fashion, as the team lost 1-0 at home to Everton.[clxxviii] But it didn't take long for the team to turn its fortunes around. The team won 5-2 in its next game[clxxix] against Southampton. Son Heung-min scored 4, but Kane set up all of them before scoring the last one for Tottenham. His South Korean teammate was quick to praise him for the performance and their relationship in the team:

"To score my first Premier League hat trick for the Spurs is a big honor for me ... I'm grateful to have this opportunity, grateful to my teammates and especially Harry, it was an amazing performance from him and he's an amazing person. What can I say? I'm very happy. I'm very proud and very grateful ...The relationship between me and Harry, it's now six seasons together, we know each other on and off the pitch. It's not perfect, we have to work on it, and we do work hard on it. I want to give more assistance to Harry as well."[clxxx]

Kane kept up this run when he scored twice against Manchester United and provided an assist in Tottenham's historic 6-1 victory at Old Trafford.[clxxxi] He produced a performance with as many goals as assists in the 3-3 draw against West Ham.[clxxxii] This led the team to new heights in the table, as they climbed to the top of the Premier League standings after defeating Manchester City 2-0.[clxxxiii]

Jose Mourinho decided to rotate his team throughout the entire group stage of the UEFA Europa League, meaning that Kane was limited to a few appearances off the bench in this phase of the competition. He was able to score his 200th goal for Tottenham,[clxxxiv] inspiring the team to defeat Ludogorets Razgrad 3-1 in Bulgaria. As anticipated, Spurs topped Group J and advanced to the next round.

Meanwhile, the team would also make steady progress in the cup as it navigated the fourth-round tie against Chelsea, defeating them via a penalty shootout[clxxxv] that saw Kane scoring the decisive spot kick. The team would go on to defeat Stoke City and Brentford in the following rounds to reach the final.

The League Cup final is traditionally held in February of the season, however, because fans were still not readily allowed into grounds during the season, a collective decision was made to move it back to late April[clxxxvi] in hopes that the virus would be weaker and less transmissible and allow a greater number of fans to attend the game.

Tottenham's form started well in the month of December in the Premier League, as did Kane personally. Scoring and assisting in the North London derby[clxxxvii] truly cemented him as a pillar of success in the fixture with his team winning 2-0. However, the results soon began to sour, and their position at the top of the Premier League began to fall. The team failed to win in its next four games to close the year. In the process, they dropped as low as eighth in a very congested table.

Entering the new year in 2021, Tottenham appeared to have just the tonic for that losing streak when they dispensed with Leeds United with a romping 3-0 display.[clxxxviii] Kane scored in that game as well as in the subsequent games against Fulham and Sheffield United. These results bolstered their position back up the league standings.

But February was another troubling time for Mourinho when Kane picked up another ankle injury,[clxxxix] ruling him out for three games. While the team was able to mount a 4-1 win in Budapest against Wolfsberger AC[cxc] without him, they succumbed to consecutive Premier League defeats against Brighton and Chelsea.

After returning from this relatively minor ankle injury, Harry made an impact in the game against West Bromwich Albion when he scored his 13th goal of the season. However, Tottenham was unable to put a run of good performances together. They suffered two losses even with Kane back on the team. And while the three following games resulted in three victories, these were against bottom-dwelling teams. Thus, concerns were raised that Tottenham could not challenge at the top end of the table, obviously as the owner desired. In that run, Kane did provide a class performance against Crystal Palace as he played a major part in all four goals in the 4-1 win.[cxci]

Tottenham would go on to win the following leg against the Austrian team, Wolfsberger AC, comfortably proceeding on an 8-1 aggregate score[cxcii] even with Kane sitting on the bench for the second match. In the last 16, Spurs were drawn against Croatian team Dinamo Zagreb. The first leg went according to plan. Harry scored twice at Tottenham Hotspur Stadium to put the North London team in control of the tie[cxciii] with a 2-0 advantage.

The return leg at Maksimir Stadium in Zagreb was not quite the expected result. Mislav Orsic did Kane one better on the night by scoring two goals in 90 minutes, giving Dinamo Zagreb the aggregate 3-2 win[cxciv] in the tie and ending Tottenham's European adventure.

Kane closed out the month of March with yet another goal in an away win at Villa Park with a penalty, taking his tally to 17 for the campaign. April 2021, however, would be a defining period for the club. While Harry continued to play well, the results were inconsistent. He scored two in the 2-2 draw with Newcastle United and another couple in yet another 2-2 result with Everton. Daniel Levy decided that, in the totality of a failure to win games and the manner of the UEFA Europa League exit, it was best to cut ties with Jose Mourinho[cxcv] and appointed Ryan Mason as the interim boss until the end of the season.

While the appointment might not have worked out as a beneficial move for the club, Harry Kane has since noted that he thoroughly enjoyed working with the prolific manager: "Jose's got so much experience in the biggest of games at the biggest of clubs and that's what I mean by saying we had a similar mentality in that aspect in doing anything to win. And that's the game. Jose just wanted to win…That was the mentality he was trying to put into the players at Spurs, do anything to win and I think like you said we did become more streetwise, but maybe there was relationships that didn't quite work there but from my point of view, he was great for me."[cxcvi]

The timing of the decision was odd. Tottenham was just days away from the League Cup final at Wembley. Therefore, one of Ryan Mason's first games in charge of the team would be a cup final against Manchester City. However, no beginners' luck was on offer, as Man City collected the trophy[cxcvii] via a 1-0 win.

Kane would play five of the six remaining Premier League games under the interim manager. He scored two goals as Tottenham finished a lowly seventh in the league standings. The player himself scored 23 goals, enough to earn him the Golden Boot for a third time.[cxcviii]

2021-22: Initial Transfer Request

Now firmly engrained in the fabric of Premier League royalty and a three-time Golden Boot winner, Harry Kane began to question whether he should still be playing for Tottenham Hotspur, a team that had not provided him with any trophies. Furthermore, Tottenham's seventh-place finish in the prior season meant that they would play in the newly formed UEFA Conference League, two steps below the Champions League.

Subsequently, he handed in a transfer request to the Tottenham board,[cxcix] officially stating his desire to leave the club. While initially entertaining the prospect of joining either Manchester United or Manchester City, Kane was convinced by the club's higher management (including Daniel Levy) to stay[cc] at the club.

Kane later took to social media to comment on his decision. "I will be staying at Tottenham this summer and will be 100% focused on helping the team achieve success. #COYS"[cci]

One of the key reasons for his change of heart could have been the appointment of Nuno Espirito Santo,[ccii] who had left Wolverhampton Wanderers with remarkable success.

The Portuguese coach started well as the team defeated Manchester City 1-0[cciii] on the opening weekend of the season. Two subsequent wins despite no Harry Kane goals still buoyed the club's league standing.

Tottenham were not automatically in the UEFA Europa Conference League, as they had to qualify via the final playoff round against Pacos Ferreira. Kane did not travel for the away leg as the team lost 1-0. However, he took the captain's armband for the match at home and scored twice in the 3-0 win[cciv] to ensure that the club would at least start its European campaign for the season.

In the Premier League, it took Kane until the middle of October to score his first goal in the competition. He came up with a match-winning performance against Newcastle United in a storied 3-2 win[ccv] at St James' Park. However, the next three games proved to be a turning point for the club as they lost to both West Ham United and Manchester United as well as only drawing with Everton. Daniel Levy decided that the style of play didn't suit Kane, who scored just once in the league under

Nuno Espirito Santos, and determined that it was again time for a change in personnel. Santos was sacked[ccvi] on November 1st.

Antonio Conte was chosen as the new head coach and stepped into the managerial position the day after Santos had departed. [ccvii] Kane may have initially struggled under all the changes, but he found a rhythm in the Premier League with his goal against Liverpool in a 2-2 draw. That led him to two more games with goals, but this meant that by the end of 2021, Kane was unusually short on Premier League goals, having scored just four.

On the continent, the team was drawn against Stade Rennais, NS Mura, and Vitesse. Tottenham started the Group G phase with a draw against the French club. Kane was most prominent in the game against the Slovenian team, NS Mura, netting a hat-trick in just 31 minutes in a 5-1 victory.[ccviii] Kane wasn't part of the next match when Tottenham lost the game against Vitesse in the Netherlands. The following two fixtures led to another loss and a win, leaving the group wide open.

The last game of the phase was supposed to be played against Stade Rennais in North London, however, Tottenham refused to participate because they had contracted multiple cases of COVID-19 at the time. The French team refused to acknowledge the revisions,[ccix] as they believed Tottenham still had enough players to contest the tie and cited a lack of sportsmanship, further noting that the team had already arrived in London by the time Tottenham tried to cancel. Hence, no game took place and UEFA later ruled that Rennes would be awarded a 3-0 win[ccx] at Tottenham's expense because they concluded that the club could have fielded a team. This decision would ultimately send the club out of the competition, and they finished third in the group.

While the inconsistencies in continental competition continued, Kane was playing a big part in Tottenham's League Cup run. In their first match of the campaign, he scored in the 2-2 draw against Wolverhampton Wanderers before scoring in the penalty shoot-out, which Tottenham won[ccxi] to advance to the next round. Spurs then advanced to the semi-final of the tournament by also defeating Burnley and West Ham United.

2022 symbolized a new beginning for the club, as Conte would try to get the team back into the UEFA Champions League as well as challenge for domestic silverware along the way in the two cup competitions. Consecutive wins against Watford, Morecambe, and Leicester City got Kane firing as they earned six points in the league, propelling them through to the next round of the FA Cup.

Of course, it was only a matter of time until Antonio Conte's former employers and London rivals to Spurs, Chelsea FC, would spoil the party. The 2-0 loss at Stamford Bridge sent them on a small losing streak in the league of three games. The team would also play Chelsea twice in the League Cup two-legged semi-final tie, losing both games[ccxii] as they suffered defeat three times to their rivals in the same calendar month.

Kane was able to inspire the team victory in the FA Cup against Brighton when he netted twice in a 3-1 win,[ccxiii] taking them to the fifth round in the club's last realistic chance at a trophy for the season. But that proved to be another pipe dream as the team was dumped out in said round by lower league opposition. Middlesbrough mustered a 1-0 win[ccxiv] after extra time.

While Conte had improved the team's output and made them into a more attractive proposition, the team remained very inconsistent. This led to a 3-2 win at Etihad Stadium,[ccxv] with Kane notably scoring a last-gasp winner against the league leaders, Manchester City, but in the same week losing 1-0 to Burnley,[ccxvi] summing up their season in a microcosm.

Kane would then go on to score five goals in the next four games in the league. This led him to make five assists in the next three games in a very productive sequence for the player.

Kane wrapped up the campaign with good goal-scoring, which included a brace[ccxvii] in the 3-0 North London derby win.[ccxviii]

Harry finished the season with 17 goals, 6 behind his teammate, Son Heung-min, who shared the Golden Boot that season with Liverpool's Mohamed Salah. More importantly, however, Tottenham finished fourth in the league standings and qualified for the illustrious UEFA Champions League again.

2022-23: Goals Up, Position Down

Even though Kane did not score in the prior pre-season, the Englishman was in fine form in their 2022-23 summer games. He found the net twice in the match against Team K League,[ccxix] as well as scoring against both Sevilla and Glasgow Rangers.

The striker firmly dismantled the August goal myth this season when he scored four goals in three games and the Spurs came out of the gate with explosive form. This run saw Kane score a multitude of important goals, carrying the team unbeaten in the league until the start of October.

While Kane played every minute of Tottenham's UEFA Champions League group stage campaign, he wasn't nearly as prolific with his performances in the Premier League. In total, he scored just one goal. However, Tottenham still qualified for the knockout round with relative ease as Group D winners.[ccxx] Tottenham suffered an early exit in the League Cup as the team lost 2-0 to Nottingham Forest at the City Ground.

Tottenham prospered in the league, climbing as high as fourth in the table after defeating Leeds United 4-3.[ccxxi] After this game, Kane and many other Tottenham players left the team to play at the FIFA World Cup in Qatar.

Despite the disappointment of the England national team, Kane returned to Tottenham in goal-scoring form, even if Spurs only managed a 2-2 draw with Brentford on Boxing Day when the league resumed.

Kane continued to be a thorn in opposition defenders' sides even with Son Heung-min not being as good as he was in his prior season. However, in totality, the team began to struggle to keep up with the Premier League elite, losing to both Arsenal and Manchester City in the same week.

In February 2023, Harry Kane accomplished a major feat for Spurs as he became the record all-time goal scorer for the club, even surpassing the 266-tally held by club legend Jimmy Greaves. His record-breaking 267th net-bustling strike came against Manchester City[ccxxii] in a 1-0 victory. While in isolation this result was marvelous, they followed it up losing 4-1 to

Leicester City,[ccxxiii] who were in the relegation zone at the time. This again brought concerns that the team was unable to perform consistently at the highest level.

The team's misery was only compounded by being knocked out of the UEFA Champions League by AC Milan when the Italians won 1-0 on aggregate.[ccxxiv] The performance was more upsetting for Spurs fans and pundits because the team looked unwilling to fix the 15-year trophyless run with an outing that barely saw them get out of second gear.

Harry Kane continued to provide heroic performances for the club in the Premier League, scoring against Chelsea and even getting two against Nottingham Forest as the team tried to salvage the season by finishing as high as they could. Kane scored in the infamous 3-3 draw at Southampton, however, the game was more memorable for Conte's post-match rant in which he lambasted the players and the owner of the club. This led to his dismissal[ccxxv] from the role in late March. From this point, interim managers took over the first team coaching and managerial duties.

Kane would go on to score nine goals in the club's last 10 games of the Premier League season, as he kept up an impressive personal season with the club falling behind his performances. Most notably, he scored the only goal in the 6-1 loss to Newcastle United,[ccxxvi] a result that would become his biggest defeat in a Tottenham shirt. Kane scored two on the final day of the season against Leeds United in a 4-1 win,[ccxxvii] in a game that saw the opposition relegated to the second tier.

Kane finished with 30 goals in the league competition, only behind Erling Haaland, who had scored 36 for Manchester City. Despite Kane's impressive goal tally, the results were not nearly as good as his performances. Spurs finished eighth in the league, meaning that in the 2023-24 season, the team would have no continental football, the first time that had happened since the 2009-10 campaign. As a result, Kane's future at the club would again come under question as clubs like Chelsea, Manchester United, and even Bayern Munich all appeared as early contenders to take him away from Tottenham Hotspur.

Chapter 4: International Career

Serving as the England captain for many years now, Harry Kane is regarded as a national hero for the Three Lions. He has remained a consistent source of goals for England, with the team qualifying for all major tournaments during his tenure in the team. Now as England's all-time top goal scorer, Kane is just missing some international awards.

England U17

Kane's international career started in the U17 category in 2010. However, this wasn't a prolific sequence for the striker, as his time with this team was limited to just 37 minutes in a substitute appearance in the U17 Algarve Tournament against Portugal, which ended 0-0. After that, he was never called upon to this specific youth category again.

England U19

The U19 system proved to be altogether more fruitful when Noel Blake handed him his first appearance at this level. Kane scored twice on his U19 debut against the representative team from Albania in a game that ended 6-1 to England.

Kane was selected for the squad that played in the UEFA U19 Championship in 2012 in Estonia. While he scored in the group stage against France, he sat on the bench in the semi-final match, as England was sent home by an impressive Greek team that won 2-1 in extra time.

England U20

The England U20 was another of Kane's short stints within the various levels of the English games. In 2013, he played in all three group stage games at the U20 World Cup in Turkey. The team did not win a single match, despite Harry's goal against Chile, and the England youngsters were again sent home without a trophy. Kane would never feature at this level again.

England U21

Kane's time with the England U21 squad was limited due to his first-team commitments with Tottenham and his early season injury issues, which stopped him from making a lot of appearances. He did, however, score a hat-trick on his full debut for the team, albeit against San Marino.

The aforementioned match was part of the UEFA U21 Championship qualifying phase as the team looked to qualify for another youth tournament. He went on to score more important goals to achieve qualification. Kane again played every minute in the group stage at the tournament, but England was again dumped out at the group stage.

Senior England Team

Harry Kane's first appearance in the senior England team came when Roy Hodgson brought him off the bench in a European Championship qualifier against Lithuania. Kane did not take long to get his England career up and running when he scored just 78 seconds[ccxxviii] after being introduced into the contest. After wrapping up the game to make it 4-0, England fans were clamoring to see Kane in an England shirt again. Kane scored in the next two competitive matches, with England easily qualifying for Euro 2016 in France.

Roy Hodgson preferred Kane[ccxxix] over his main competition, Jamie Vardy, for the primary striker role. Kane started three of the four matches (the only omission being a dead rubber). England might have navigated the group stage but lost to Iceland in the knockout round.[ccxxx] This ultimately led to Roy Hodgson stepping down from his role as England manager. Kane finished the tournament without scoring a goal.

While injuries prevented Kane from contributing to the early parts of England's 2018 World Cup qualification route, when he returned, he popped up with goals against Scotland, Malta,

Slovenia, and Lithuania. Ahead of the game at Hampden Park against Scotland, Harry took the captain's armband[ccxxxi] while the new manager, Gareth Southgate, decided on who should take it permanently after Wayne Rooney retired from international football.[ccxxxii] Kane was eventually named as the permanent replacement[ccxxxiii] ahead of the 2018 World Cup in Russia.

England played Tunisia in its opening match of the World Cup with Harry Kane scoring both goals in a 2-1 victory,[ccxxxiv] notching up his first and second major tournament goal for the team. The latter was a stoppage-time winner, encasing Kane as a real asset to the England team.

Kane's eye-catching performances didn't stop there, however. In the next game against Panama, he scored a hat-trick when England defeated Panama 6-1 to become one of the early tournament favorites with six points already on the board. After the match, Kane noted, "It's a pretty proud moment, amazing performance from the team—it's not often you get to enjoy a 5-0 lead at the World Cup … We had fun out there, we worked hard, we played well so we're enjoying it."[ccxxxv]

Kane sat on the bench as both England and Belgium had already qualified in the dead rubber match within the group. Harry would need the rest, as he would play 120 minutes in the next game when England played Colombia in the Round of 16. He scored England's go-ahead goal, but Yerry Mina was able to take the time beyond the 90. As such, a penalty shoot-out was needed after a further 30 minutes. Kane stepped up first, scored his spot kick, and England ultimately progressed to the next round[ccxxxvi] with Kane on six goals at the tournament.

In the quarter-final, England saw off Sweden 2-0 without Kane finding the net. However, the good times simply couldn't last, as England faced elimination from the tournament in the semi-final round when Croatia came from behind to defeat them. Kane finished as the tournament's top scorer and took home the golden boot[ccxxxvii] while the team lost the 3rd place playoff match to Belgium.

Despite initially struggling in the newly formed UEFA Nations League, England would win the prior two games against Spain and Croatia with Kane leading the line with three goals.[ccxxxviii] This would send England into the UEFA Nations League Finals tournament, however, they lost in the first round to the Netherlands.

The qualification campaign for the following European championship proved to be an enthralling phase for Harry

Kane's England career as he scored in all eight consecutive qualifying matches, notching 12 goals[ccxxxix] in the process.

Euro 2020 was postponed for a year due to the COVID-19 pandemic. However, England built upon the fantastic outing in 2018 as the team was efficient through the group phase. Harry Kane took until the second round to score but provided a historic goal against their bitter rivals, Germany.

After this, Kane scored two in the quarter-final match against Ukraine in Rome as England won 4-0,[ccxl] booking a spot in the semi-final at Wembley against Denmark. That match went to extra time after 90 minutes, when Harry Kane was tasked with taking a penalty for England. While the initial kick was saved, Kane was able to tap in the rebound and put England into its first major final since 1966.

Kane quickly commented after reaching the final, "We said in the build-up we can talk as much as we want about how we'd learned from 2018 but we had to show it on the pitch … It was a top performance—we had to dig in deep after the first goal we conceded in the tournament, and we regrouped well and showed good team spirit to come back and win the game … We've got one more game to go. What a fantastic tournament it's been so far."[ccxli]

Despite these improvements and the team cohesion, England could not get the better of Italy in the final. The teams went in level after 90 minutes and played out extra time, needing a penalty shoot-out to award the trophy. Kane scored on his chance but others didn't, and the team was shellshocked to lose the tournament[ccxlii] via penalties. Kane scored four goals in the tournament but it was not enough to match the tournament's top scorers (both on five), Patrik Schick and Cristiano Ronaldo.

Next up for England was to qualify for the World Cup in Qatar. Kane continued his exceptional goal tally in these qualifying excursions (albeit against weaker opposition) as England went undefeated throughout. Kane himself scored 12 again in the process, notably hitting three against Albania and four in the away game against San Marino,[ccxliii] which ended 10-0. However, his performance against Albania was remarkable as it was a "perfect hat-trick,"[ccxliv] meaning that he scored with his left foot, right foot, and head—a rare feat for even the very best footballers!

The next phase for England was to take on the UEFA Nations League A with a tricky group populated alongside Italy, Germany, and Hungary. However, given that the team had made the semi-final and a final in consecutive tournaments, there was a belief that the Three Lions would have enough to contest the group. Kane scored just twice in the six games as England failed to win throughout and was relegated[ccxlv] to the second ranking of the competition for the future edition.

Despite the speculation that Gareth Southgate was not fit to manage the England team[ccxlvi] any further, let alone in the 2022 World Cup, he was given the nod to keep his job for the tournament.

England played Iran in the first match of the tournament, where Kane set up two goals in a big 6-2 victory.[ccxlvii] England was frustrated in the second match against the USA when they were held to 0-0.[ccxlviii] Kane did, however, step up with another assist in the final group match, which saw England win 3-0 against local rivals Wales[ccxlix] to glide out of the group stage.

Kane then scored in England's 3-0 triumph against Senegal[ccl] as the nation reached the quarter-final. But this match would be a tough contest, as it was against the champions from 2018, France. Kane scored a goal to make it 1-1 in the match, however, France responded to make it 2-1.

England were then awarded an 84th-minute penalty, and Kane would be facing his Tottenham Hotspur teammate again as he stepped up for the responsibility. He uncharacteristically missed the penalty,[ccli] which essentially saw the French proceed and England go home.

Kane reflected that the miss would trouble him forever: "After it happened, I just wanted to play again as quickly as possible and get it out of my head. It's something you have to deal with … I'll probably remember it for the rest of my life, but that's part of the game. It's not going to affect me as a player or as a person. I'll keep working hard to improve."[cclii]

England then continued its empathetic record in qualifying by winning all four matches after being knocked out of the World Cup, with England scoring against Italy and Ukraine in March. In June 2023, Harry Kane made history in an England shirt as he scored his 54th goal for the national team with a successful spot kick against Malta.[i] This eclipsed the previous record held by Wayne Rooney for multiple years.

Chapter 5: Personal Life

Harry Kane is well-known to be one of the less flashy and well-grounded footballers when not on the pitch, keeping his personal life relatively private. Rather than go out drinking like many of his counterparts, Kane has often said that he likes nothing more than drinking tea and relaxing by watching TV shows like Dexter or the NFL[ccliii] on a Sunday if his schedule permits. Kane has told media outlets that most of his friends and family, including his wife, just refer to him as "H."[ccliv]

More recently, Kane has noted that he enjoys playing video games, especially Fortnite.[cclv] In fact, he even worked with EA Sports on FIFA 17 as an authenticity consultant[cclvi] when they crafted a new story mode on the video game franchise. As well as being a professional footballer, Kane also enjoys playing golf recreationally. His celebrity status and relatively good swing led him to be invited to play at the Icons Series.[cclvii]

Kane married his childhood sweetheart, Kate Goodland[cclviii] in June 2019. The couple have since had three children together. Katie is well revered by football fans as a very supportive figure for Harry, notably having been seen comforting her husband after England lost the Euro 2022 final[cclix] on penalties. Kane's family also extends to a few canine members. He's known to have multiple dogs and enjoys walking them in his free time.

The player has often been seen as an advocate for mental health awareness. He has made contributions to charities concerned with the matter as well as launching the Harry Kane Foundation,[cclx] a charitable firm that tries to remove the stigma from mental health.

Chapter 6: Future and Legacy

At the end of the 2022-23 season, Harry Kane is seen as one of the best footballers in both the collective histories of Tottenham Hotspur and the England national team. His determination, demeanor, and raw goal tally have ensured him this prestige, despite winning nothing on the football field other than individual accolades and a few minor pre-season tournaments. Kane was, however, rewarded for services to football by the British monarchy as he was awarded an MBE[iii] in March 2019.

The destination in which he will play his football remains uncertain as of the summer of 2023. Every team under the sun would want to sign a player like Harry, while Tottenham will try to get him to re-sign with the club. However, the lack of continental football may be very unappealing to the player.

Kane has already scored 213 goals in the Premier League.[cclxi] If he stays in England, it is widely expected that he will one day become the all-time Premier League top scorer[cclxii] by surpassing Alan Shearer's 260 record. Some have even predicted that Kane could do this by 2025 if he keeps up at the same rate of goals. However, if he moves to Bayern Munich (one of the primary parties interested in signing him) that particular project may be put on hold. But no matter what pitch he lands on, you can bet we'll be tuning in to watch.

Final Word/About the Author

I was born and raised in Norwalk, Connecticut. Growing up, I could often be found spending many nights watching basketball, soccer, and football matches with my father in the family living room. I love sports and everything that sports can embody. I believe that sports are one of the most genuine forms of competition, heart, and determination. I write my works to learn more about influential athletes in the hopes that from my writing, you the reader can walk away inspired to put in an equal if not greater amount of hard work and perseverance to pursue your goals. If you enjoyed *Harry Kane: The Inspiring Story of One of Soccer's Star Strikers,* please leave a review! Also, you can read more of my works on *David Ortiz, Cody Bellinger, Alex Bregman, Francisco Lindor, Shohei Ohtani, Ronald Acuna Jr., Javier Baez, Jose Altuve, Christian Yelich, Max Scherzer, Mookie Betts, Pete Alonso, Clayton Kershaw, Mike Trout, Bryce Harper, Jackie Robinson, Justin Verlander, Derek Jeter, Ichiro Suzuki, Ken Griffey Jr., Babe Ruth, Aaron Judge, Novak Djokovic, Roger Federer, Rafael Nadal, Serena Williams, Naomi Osaka, Coco Gauff, Baker Mayfield, George Kittle, Matt Ryan, Matthew Stafford, Eli Manning, Khalil Mack, Davante Adams, Terry Bradshaw, Jimmy Garoppolo, Philip Rivers, Von Miller, Aaron Donald, Joey Bosa, Josh Allen, Mike*

Evans, Joe Burrow, Carson Wentz Adam Thielen, Stefon Diggs,
Lamar Jackson, Dak Prescott, Patrick Mahomes, Odell
Beckham Jr., J.J. Watt, Colin Kaepernick, Aaron Rodgers, Tom
Brady, Russell Wilson, Peyton Manning, Drew Brees, Calvin
Johnson, Brett Favre, Rob Gronkowski, Andrew Luck, Richard
Sherman, Bill Belichick, Candace Parker, Skylar Diggins-
Smith, A'ja Wilson, Lisa Leslie, Sue Bird, Diana Taurasi, Julius
Erving, Clyde Drexler, John Havlicek, Oscar Robertson, Ja
Morant, Gary Payton, Khris Middleton, Michael Porter Jr.,
Julius Randle, Jrue Holiday, Domantas Sabonis, Mike Conley
Jr., Jerry West, Dikembe Mutombo, Fred VanVleet, Jamal
Murray, Zion Williamson, Brandon Ingram, Jaylen Brown,
Charles Barkley, Trae Young, Andre Drummond, JJ Redick,
DeMarcus Cousins, Wilt Chamberlain, Bradley Beal, Rudy
Gobert, Aaron Gordon, Kristaps Porzingis, Nikola Vucevic,
Andre Iguodala, Devin Booker, John Stockton, Jeremy Lin,
Chris Paul, Pascal Siakam, Jayson Tatum, Gordon Hayward,
Nikola Jokic, Bill Russell, Victor Oladipo, Luka Doncic, Ben
Simmons, Shaquille O'Neal, Joel Embiid, Donovan Mitchell,
Damian Lillard, Giannis Antetokounmpo, Chris Bosh, Kemba
Walker, Isaiah Thomas, DeMar DeRozan, Amar'e Stoudemire,
Al Horford, Yao Ming, Marc Gasol, Draymond Green, Kawhi
Leonard, Dwyane Wade, Ray Allen, Pau Gasol, Dirk Nowitzki,

Jimmy Butler, Paul Pierce, Manu Ginobili, Pete Maravich, Larry Bird, Kyle Lowry, Jason Kidd, David Robinson, LaMarcus Aldridge, Derrick Rose, Paul George, Kevin Garnett, Michael Jordan, LeBron James, Kyrie Irving, Klay Thompson, Stephen Curry, Kevin Durant, Russell Westbrook, Chris Paul, Blake Griffin, Kobe Bryant, Anthony Davis, Joakim Noah, Scottie Pippen, Carmelo Anthony, Kevin Love, Grant Hill, Tracy McGrady, Vince Carter, Patrick Ewing, Karl Malone, Tony Parker, Allen Iverson, Hakeem Olajuwon, Reggie Miller, Michael Carter-Williams, James Harden, John Wall, Tim Duncan, Steve Nash, Gregg Popovich, Pat Riley, John Wooden, Steve Kerr, Brad Stevens, Red Auerbach, Doc Rivers, Erik Spoelstra, Mike D'Antoni, and *Phil Jackson* in the Kindle Store. If you love soccer, check out my website at claytongeoffreys.com to join my exclusive list where I let you know about my latest books and give you lots of goodies.

Like what you read? Please leave a review!

I write because I love sharing the stories of influential athletes like Harry Kane with fantastic readers like you. My readers inspire me to write more so please do not hesitate to let me know what you thought by leaving a review! If you love books on life, soccer, or productivity, check out my website at claytongeoffreys.com to join my exclusive list where I let you know about my latest books. Aside from being the first to hear about my latest releases, you can also download a free copy of *33 Life Lessons: Success Principles, Career Advice & Habits of Successful People.* See you there!

Clayton

References

[i] Sky News. Harry Kane becomes England men's record goal scorer after scoring against Italy. Sky. 24 March 2023. Web.

[ii] Holt, Oliver: He's had no place among the Messi and Ronaldo-led fake smiles at the Ballon d'Or but Harry Kane is our unfashionable great. It's time he finally gets real recognition as the LEGEND he is. The Daily Mail. 24 January 2023. Web.

[iii] Sky News. Harry Kane receives MBE for services to football after World Cup exploits. Sky. 28 March 2019. Web.

[iv] Tottenham Hotspur. Kane Awarded Freedom of the City of London. Tottenham Hotspur. 26 May 2023. Web.

[v] Hynter, David. 'Not good enough': Harry Kane's verdict on another trophyless Spurs season. The Guardian. 9 March 2023. Web.

[vi] Blow, Tom. Exclusive: Adorable Harry Kane childhood snap shows how England's 'KO-King' honed skills used today. The Mirror. 6 December 2022. Web.

[vii] Fay, Sean. Tottenham's Harry Kane Explains Viral Picture of Him in an Arsenal Shirt Aged 8. Bleacher Report. 2 February 2015. Web.

[viii] Hoskin, Rob. Harry Kane: Is Spurs legend actually an Arsenal fan? Give Me Sport. 6 February 2023. Web.

[ix] Mullock, Simon. Exclusive: Harry Kane's love for Arsenal laid bare as history-changing offer revealed. The Mirror. 15 April 2023. Web.

[x] Kane, Harry. Harry Kane's grassroots story. England Football. 23 March 2023. Web.

[xi] Sports Illustrated. Former Teammate Reveals Why Harry Kane Was Released From Arsenal's Academy. Sports Illustrated. 27 September 2018. Web.

[xii] Berrill, Lewis. Harry Kane, Bukayo Saka and Jadon Sancho's time at Watford FC. Watford Observer. 9 July 2021. Web.

[xiii] Gray, Harry. Harry Kane: Tottenham Hotspur striker reveals how Watford helped launch his career. Watford Observer. 5 February 2018. Web.

[xiv] Planet Sport. Harry Kane Profile. Planet Sport. 2023. Web.

[xv] Stafford-Bloor, Seb. Where Are They Now? Tottenham's 2007/08 League Cup-winning squad. Four Four Two. 5 January 2017. Web.

[xvi] BBC Sport. Tottenham 2-0 Everton. BBC. 27 October 2009. Web.

[xvii] Roopanarine, Les. Tottenham 4-0 Bolton. BBC Sport. 24 February 2010. Web.

[xviii] O'Connor, Robert. Inside the Loan Spells of Harry Kane from Those Who Were There. Bleacher Report. 6 September 2017. Web.

xix Howard, Derren. The Brighton and Leyton Orient Assist King Who Set-Up Harry Kane's First Ever Professional Goal. Sussex World. 24 March 2023. Web.

xx BBC Sport. Leyton Orient 4-0 Sheffield Wednesday. BBC. 22 January 2011. Web.

xxi BBC Sport. Leyton Orient 4-1 Bristol Rovers. BBC. 12 February 2011. Web.

xxii BBC Sport. Harry Kane sponsors Leyton Orient shirts for third season. BBC. 22 June 2022. Web.

xxiii Murray, Ewan. Five things we learned from Hearts 0 Tottenham Hotspur 5. The Guardian. 18 August 2011. Web.

xxiv Doyle, Paul. Hearts salvage pride as Tottenham progress to Europa League group stage. The Guardian. 25 August 2011. Web.

xxv Highet, Lochlin. Jamie MacDonald recalls Harry Kane penalty save and hopes experience helps in Europa League. The Daily Record. 11 July 2019. Web.

xxvi Tottenham Hotspur. We were there... team-mates recall Harry Kane's first goal for Spurs in 2011. Tottenham Hotspur. 9 February 2023. Web.

xxvii Pettit, Mark. Resounding Spurs win at Rovers in vain. UEFA Europa League. 15 December 2011. Web.

xxviii Harte, Declan. 3 players you probably forgot ever put on a Millwall shirt. Football League World. 4 November 2022. Web.

xxix The Guardian. Nicky Maynard strikes late for Bristol City to punish Millwall. The Guardian. 4 January 2012. Web.

xxx BBC Sport. Marlon King scored twice as Birmingham City underlined their promotion credentials with a 6-0 thrashing of nine-man Millwall at The New Den. BBC. 14 January 2012. Web.

xxxi Black, Dan. PHOTOS: Burnley 1, Millwall 3. The Burnley Express. 27 February 2012. Web.

xxxii The Daily Mail. Peterborough 0 Millwall 3: Posh mauled by Lions' treble. The Daily Mail. 6 March 2012. Web.

xxxiii George-Miller, Dustin. Kane: 2012 Millwall loan "turned me into a man". Cartilage Free Captain. 9 March 2017. Web.

xxxiv BBC Sport. Norwich City sign Harry Kane on season loan from Tottenham. BBC. 1 September 2012. Web.

xxxv Smallwood, Jimmy. Norwich are still searching for their first win of the season after a goalless draw with West Ham. BBC Sport. 15 September 2012. Web.

xxxvi Sky Sports. On-loan Tottenham striker Harry Kane will miss two months with a broken metatarsal, Norwich have confirmed. Sky. 28

September 2012. Web.

xxxvii The Independent. Tottenham recall striker Harry Kane from Norwich. The Independent. 1 February 2013. Web.

xxxviii Austen-Hardy, Patrick. Harry Kane "couldn't hold the ball up" during forgotten Premier League loan spell. The Daily Star. 6 June 2022. Web.

xxxix Perrin, Charles. Spurs send Harry Kane on loan to Leicester. The Express. 25 February 2013. Web.

xl Percy, John. Leicester City 3 Blackburn Rovers 0: match report. The Telegraph. 26 February 2013. Web.

xli Sanghera, Mandeep. Watford 3-1 Leicester (agg 3-2). BBC Sport. 12 May 2013. Web.

xlii Spencer, Phil. LOVES IT Harry Kane continues staggering goalscoring record against Leicester as Tottenham star hits 20th strike against Foxes. Talk Sport. 17 September 2023. Web.

xliii The Daily Mail. Monaco 5 Tottenham 2: Spurs feeling effects without Bale as Falcao and Co run riot. The Daily Mail. 3 August 2013. Web.

xliv Steinberg, Jacob. Monaco 5-2 Tottenham Hotspur – as it happened. The Guardian. 3 August 2013. Web.

xlv Tighe, Sam. Tottenham Hotspur vs. Dinamo Tbilisi: Score, Grades and Post-Match Reaction. Bleacher Report. 29 August 2013. Web.

xlvi McCauley, Kim. Tottenham Hotspur vs. Hull City: Final score 2-2, Spurs advance on penalties. Cartilage Free Captain. 30 October 2013. Web.

xlvii BBC Sport. Tottenham Hotspur 2-2 Hull City. BBC. 30 October 2013. Web.

xlviii Hynter, David. Spurs make Tim Sherwood full-time head coach on 18-month contract. The Guardian. 23 December 2013. Web.

xlix Eurosport. Tim Sherwood: I Am Responsible For Harry Kane's Development. Eurosport. 3 February 2015. Web.

l Scott-Eliot, Robin. Tottenham 5 Sunderland 1: Tim Sherwood wields Harry Kane to thrash Sunderland at White Hart Lane. The Independent. 8 April 2014. Web.

li Prince-Wright, Joe. West Bromwich Albion 3-3 Tottenham Hotspur: Sensational Spurs fight back (video). NBC Sports. 12 April 2014. Web.

lii Reich, Josh. Tottenham 3 Fulham 1: Harry Kane scores again as Spurs keep top four hopes alive. The Evening Standard. 19 April 2014. Web.

liii Jurejko, Jonathan. Tottenham Hotspur 3-1 Dnipropetrovsk. BBC Sport. 27 February 2014. Web.

liv McCauley, Kim. Benfica vs. Tottenham Hotspur: Final score 2-2, Spurs come up just short. Cartilage Free Captain. 20 March 2013. Web.

lv Magowan, Alistair. Benfica 2-2 Tottenham Hotspur. BBC Sport. 20 March

2014. Web.

lvi The Guardian. Mauricio Pochettino confirmed as Tottenham manager on five-year deal. The Guardian. 27 May 2014. Web.

lvii Rooke, Sam. Chicago Fire 0, Tottenham 2: 6 Things We Learned from Spurs Friendly. Bleacher Report. 27 July 2014. Web.

lviii Four Four Two. Tottenham hit Celtic for six in Finland friendly. Four Four Two Magazine. 2 August 2014. Web.

lix West Ham United. FT - West Ham United 0-1 Tottenham. West Ham United. 16 August 2014. Web.

lx Peck, Tom. Tottenham Hotspur vs AEL Limassol Europa League match report: Harry Kane proves Spurs' perfect citizen. The Independent. 29 August 2019. Web.

lxi Cummings, Michael. Tottenham Hotspur vs Asteras: Score, Grades and Reaction from Europa League Game. Bleacher Report. 23 October 2014. Web.

lxii Canavan, Steve. Tottenham Hotspur 5-1 Asteras Tripolis. BBC Sport. 23 October 2014. Web.

lxiii UEFA Europa League. Beşiktaş beat Tottenham to top Group C. UEFA. 11 December 2014. Web.

lxiv Whalley, Mark. Aston Villa 1-2 Tottenham Hotspur. BBC Sport. 2 November 2014. Web.

lxv Kilpatrick, David. Harry Kane goal vs Aston Villa in 2014 saved my job - Spurs' Pochettino. ESPN. 15 September 2017. Web.

lxvi Cryer, Andy. Leicester City 1-2 Tottenham Hotspur. BBC Sport. 26 December 2014. Web.

lxvii Wilkinson, Jack. Premier League: Tottenham beat Chelsea 5-3 at White Hart Lane. Sky Sports. 1 January 2015. Web.

lxviii Nursey, James. West Brom 0-3 Tottenham: Harry Kane nets twice as classy Spurs claim three points. The Mirror. 31 January 2015. Web.

lxix Harris, Chris. Tottenham Hotspur 2-1 Arsenal – Report. Arsenal. 7 February 2015. Web.

lxx Tottenham Hotspur. The King in the North. Tottenham Hotspur. 2022. Web.

lxxi Smith, Alan. Football Clockwatch: QPR 1-2 Tottenham, Football League and more – as it happened. The Guardian. 7 March 2015. Web.

lxxii Gheerbant, James. Fiorentina 2-0 Tottenham Hotspur. BBC Sport. 26 February 2015. Web.

lxxiii Hynter, David. Tottenham's Harry Kane bags hat-trick in thriller against Leicester. The Guardian. 21 March 2015. Web.

lxxiv Anderson, David. Harry Kane declares it's been "the best week of my life" despite Tottenham's bore draw at Burnley. The Irish Mirror. 5 April 2015. Web.

lxxv George-Miller, Dustin. Tottenham 1-2 Leicester: Spurs crash out of FA Cup after loss to EPL cellar-dwellers. Cartilage Free Captain. 24 January 2014. Web.

lxxvi Rostance, Tom. Sheffield United 2-2 Tottenham Hotspur. BBC Sport. 28 January 2015. Web.

lxxvii Higgins, Adam. The First Time We Beat Spurs At Wembley. Manchester United. 10 January 2019. Web.

lxxviii Olley, Declan. Tottenham's 2008 League Cup win: Former Spurs captain Ledley King revisits club's last trophy 14 years on. Sky Sports. 25 February 2022. Web.

lxxix McNulty, Phil. Chelsea 2-0 Tottenham Hotspur. BBC Sport. 1 March 2015. Web.

lxxx Maltby, Matt. Harry Kane named PFA Young Player of the Year 2015: Tottenham striker beats off stiff competition to cap off 'unreal' season. The Daily Mail. 26 April 2015. Web.

lxxxi Fox Sports. PFA team of the year 2014-15: Chelsea dominate the XI, but no room for Cesc Fabregas. Fox. 27 April 2015. Web.

lxxxii Zainal, Zulhilmi. Malaysia XI 1-2 Tottenham Hotspur: Easy win for the Londoners. Goal. 2 June 2015. Web.

lxxxiii Borg, Simon. MLS All-Stars 2, Tottenham Hotspur 1 | 2015 AT&T MLS All-Star Game. Major League Soccer. 30 July 2015. Web.

lxxxiv The Guardian. Tottenham confirm signing of Son Heung-min from Bayer Leverkusen. The Guardian. 28 August 2015. Web.

lxxxv Eccleshare, Charlie. How Kane and Son became one of the best partnerships in Premier League history. The Athletic. 23 February 2022. Web.

lxxxvi ESPN. Tottenham top Anderlecht, move atop Group J thanks to Dembele strike. ESPN. 17 May 2023. Web.

lxxxvii Chowdhury, Saj. FK Qarabag 0-1 Tottenham Hotspur. BBC Sport. 26 November 2015. Web.

lxxxviii Higginson, Marc. Tottenham Hotspur 4-1 Monaco. BBC Sport. 10 December 2015. Web.

lxxxix Newman, Stuart. Tottenham vs. Manchester City: Score and Reaction from 2015 Premier League Match. Bleacher Report. 26 September 2015. Web.

xc Bennett, Tom. Harry Kane Hits Hat-Trick As Tottenham Thrash Struggling Bournemouth. Eurosport. 25 October 2015. Web.

xci Thomas, Lyall. Tottenham 1-2 Arsenal: Mathieu Flamini scores twice in north London derby. Sky Sports. 24 September 2015. Web.

[xcii] Surlis, Patrick. Tottenham Hotspur 2-2 Leicester City: Late Harry Kane penalty earns replay. Sky Sports. 11 January 2016. Web.

[xciii] Cryer, Andy. Tottenham Hotspur 2-2 Leicester City. BBC Sport. 10 January 2016. Web.

[xciv] Chowdhury, Saj. Leicester City 0-2 Tottenham Hotspur. BBC Sport. 20 January 2016. Web.

[xcv] McGeehan, Matt. Colchester 1 Tottenham 4: Nacer Chadli scores twice to send Spurs into the fifth round of the FA Cup. The Evening Standard. 30 January 2016. Web.

[xcvi] ITV. FA Cup match report: Tottenham Hotspur 0-1 Crystal Palace. ITV. 21 February 2016. Web.

[xcvii] Pettit, Mark. Impressive Spurs swat Fiorentina aside. UEFA Europa League. 25 February 201t6. Web.

[xcviii] Brassell, Andy. Aubameyang spurs Dortmund to Tottenham scalp. UEFA Europa League. 17 March 2016.

[xcix] James, Josh. Arsenal 2-1 Leicester City - Match report. Arsenal. 5 February 2016. Web.

[c] McNulty, Phil. Tottenham Hotspur 2-2 Arsenal. BBC Sport. 5 March 2016. Web.

[ci] Taylor, Daniel. Tottenham burn through Stoke as Kane and Alli put heat on Leicester. The Guardian. 18 April 2016. Web.

[cii] Sunderland, Tom. Tottenham vs. West Brom: Score, Reaction from 2016 Premier League Game. Bleacher Report. 25 April 2016. Web.

[ciii] Taylor, Daniel. Leicester City's draw with Manchester United puts Premier League title on hold. The Guardian. 1 May 2016. Web.

[civ] Yew, Oliver. Chelsea 2-2 Tottenham: Eden Hazard strike ends Spurs' title hopes. Sky Sports. 3 May 2016. Web.

[cv] Lewis, Aimee. Chelsea 2-2 Tottenham Hotspur. BBC Sport. 2 May 2016. Web.

[cvi] Prenderville, Liam. Harry Kane admits Premier League Golden Boot is a "dream come true" after impressive 25-goal campaign. The Mirror. 18 May 2016. Web.

[cvii] Eurosport. Tottenham Run Riot In 6-1 Thrashing Of Inter Milan. Eurosport. 5 August 2016. Web.

[cviii] Jones, Lewis. Stoke City 0-4 Tottenham: Mark Hughes sent off in thrashing. Sky Sports. 10 September 2016. Web.

[cix] McNulty, Phil. Tottenham Hotspur 1-2 Monaco. BBC Sport. 14 September 2016. Web.

[cx] The Observer. Tottenham Hotspur to play Champions League matches at

Wembley. The Guardian. 28 May 2016. Web.

cxi Sunderland AFC. Tottenham Hotspur 1-0 Sunderland. Sunderland AFC. September 2016. Web.

cxii The Guardian. Harry Kane ankle injury leaves Tottenham fearing scan result. The Guardian. 19 September 2016. Web.

cxiii Burt, Jason. Arsenal 1 Tottenham 1: Hosts blow big chance as Harry Kane returns to snatch a draw. The Telegraph. 6 November 2016. Web.

cxiv Marsh, Charlotte. Tottenham 3-2 West Ham: Harry Kane double nicks dramatic late win. Sky Sports.

cxv Strickland, Jamie. Monaco 2-1 Tottenham Hotspur. BBC Sport. 22 November 2016. Web.

cxvi Hynter, David. Pochettino gamble falls flat in Monaco and Spurs crash out after five games. The Guardian. 22 November 2016. Web.

cxvii Verschueren, Gianni. Tottenham vs. CSKA Moscow: Score and Reaction from 2016 Champions League Match. Bleacher Report. 7 December 2016. Web.

cxviii Prince-Wright, Joe. Tottenham 5-0 Swansea: Kane, Eriksen on song to dominate Swans. NBC Sports. 3 December 2016. Web.

cxix McNulty, Phil. Tottenham Hotspur 2-0 Chelsea. BBC Sport.

cxx Surlis, Patrick. Tottenham 4-0 West Brom: Harry Kane hat-trick sends Spurs second in Premier League. Sky Sports. 14 January 2017. Web.

cxxi George-Miller, Dustin. WATCH: Hat-trick hero Harry Kane scores his third against Fulham. Cartilage Free Captain. 19 February 2017. Web.

cxxii Millwall FC. Report | Tottenham Hotspur 6-0 Millwall. Millwall FC. 12 March 2017. Web.

cxxiii BT Sport. Highlights: Tottenham 2-2 Gent (agg 2-3). BT. 23 February 2017. Web.

cxxiv Blanchette, Rob. Tottenham Beat Manchester United 2-1 in Final Match at White Hart Lane. Bleacher Report. 14 May 2017. Web.

cxxv Chapman, Caroline. Tottenham Hotspur 2-1 Manchester United. BBC Sport. 14 May 2017. Web.

cxxvi Taylor, Daniel. Chelsea win Premier League title again as Michy Batshuayi sinks West Brom. The Guardian. 12 May 2017. Web.

cxxvii Doyle, Paul. Tottenham's Harry Kane strikes four in 6-1 thrashing of Leicester. The Guardian. 18 May 2017. Web.

cxxviii Verschueren, Gianni. Chelsea Beat Tottenham Hotspur 4-2 in Spectacular FA Cup Semi-Final. Bleacher Report. 22 April 2017. Web.

cxxix Walker, Mark. Hull City 1 Tottenham 7: Harry Kane scores second hat-trick in a week as Spurs sign off in style. The Evening Standard. 21 May 2017. Web.

[cxxx] Taylor, Louise. Harry Kane hat-trick secures Golden Boot as Tottenham hit Hull for seven. The Guardian. 21 May 2017. Web.

[cxxxi] Tottenham Hotspur. Kitchee SC 1-4 Spurs. Tottenham Hotspur. 26 May 2017. Web.

[cxxxii] Richards, Alex. Tottenham confirm they will play ALL home games at Wembley in 2017-18 season. The Mirror. 28 April 2017. Web.

[cxxxiii] Tottenham Hotspur. Spurs 2-0 Juventus - report from Wembley. Tottenham Hotspur. 5 August 2017. Web.

[cxxxiv] Golson, Michael. WAKE ME UP WHEN AUGUST ENDS The stats behind Harry Kane's August goal-drought is simply incredible and proves the hoodoo is REAL. Dream Team The Sun. 11 August 2018. Web.

[cxxxv] Mendola, Nicholas. Everton 0-3 Tottenham Hotspur: Kane breaks out at Goodison. NBC Sports. 9 September 2017. Web.

[cxxxvi] The Irish Independent. Mauricio Pochettino: It's hard to describe in-form Harry Kane. The Irish Independent. 30 September 2017. Web.

[cxxxvii] Burt, Jason. Tottenham 3 Borussia Dortmund 1: Harry Kane shows his class as Spurs banish Wembley woes. The Telegraph. 13 September 2017. Web.

[cxxxviii] Brand, Gerard. Tottenham 3-1 Real Madrid: Spurs qualify for last 16 with famous win. Sky Sports. 2 November 2017. Web.

[cxxxix] Rose, Gary. Borussia Dortmund 1-2 Tottenham Hotspur. BBC Sport. 21 November 2017. Web.

[cxl] Benge, James. Tottenham 4 Liverpool 1: Harry Kane stars for Spurs as Jurgen Klopp's defence crumbles at Wembley. The Telegraph. 22 October 2017. Web.

[cxli] George-Miller, Dustin. Harry Kane to miss Manchester United match with hamstring strain. Cartilage Free Captain. 27 October 2017. Web.

[cxlii] George-Miller, Dustin. Tottenham Hotspur vs. Stoke: final score 5-1, Spurs stake Stoke with brilliant second half. Cartilage Free Captain. 9 December 2017. Web.

[cxliii] Chapman, Caroline. Tottenham Hotspur 5-2 Southampton. BBC Sport. 26 December 2017. Web.

[cxliv] McNulty, Phil. Liverpool 2-2 Tottenham Hotspur. BBC Sport. 4 February 2018. Web.

[cxlv] Thomas, Lyall. Juventus 2-2 Tottenham: Spurs fight back claims edge in last-16 tie. Sky Sports. 14 February 2018. Web.

[cxlvi] Taylor, Daniel. Juventus's Higuaín and Dybala send Tottenham spiralling out of Europe. The Guardian. 7 March 2018. Web.

[cxlvii] Rosser, Jack. Manchester United 2 Tottenham 1: Ander Herrera goal books FA Cup Final place as Spurs' semi-final hoodoo continues. The

Evening Standard. 21 April 2018. Web.

cxlviii Sports Illustrated. Tottenham to Start 2018/19 Season at Wembley Amid Fears That New Stadium Will Not Be Ready in Time. Sports Illustrated. 13 June 2018. Web.

cxlix ESPN. Tottenham win rare trophy as International Champions Cup concludes. ESPN. 11 August 2018. Web.

cl Cooke, Richard. Harry Kane relieved to end August goal drought with Tottenham. Sky Sports. 19 August 2018. Web.

cli Jones, Michael. Manchester United 0-3 Tottenham Hotspur: Harry Kane and Lucas Moura score for Spurs, as it happened. The Independent. 27 August 2018. Web.

clii James, Josh. Arsenal 0-2 Tottenham: How it happened. Arsenal. 19 December 2018. Web.

cliii Marsh, Charlotte. Tottenham 2-1 PSV: Harry Kane keeps Champions League hopes alive. Sky Sports. 7 November 2018. Web.

cliv Hynter, David. Christian Eriksen pounces to give Spurs crucial victory over Internazionale. The Guardian. 28 November 2018. Web.

clv Tranmere Rovers. Tranmere 0-7 Tottenham. Tranmere Rovers. 4 January 2019. Web.

clvi Fifield, Dominic. Tottenham lose Harry Kane until March due to ankle ligament injury. The Guardian. 15 January 2019. Web.

clvii Ashton, Neil. SPURS 3 DORTMUND 0 Son, Vertonghen and Llorente strike as Tottenham stun Germans. The Sun. 13 February 2019. Web.

clviii Reuters. Soccer-Kane scores in Dortmund as Tottenham stroll into last eight. Reuters. 5 March 2019. Web.

clix Taylor, Daniel. Son's solo effort secures win for Spurs after Lloris saves Man City penalty. The Guardian. 9 April 2019. Web.

clx Grez, Matias. Tottenham edge out Manchester City but lose Harry Kane to injury. CNN. 10 April 2019. Web.

clxi Anderson, Jamie. Man City 4-3 Tottenham: VAR disallows Sterling goal as Spurs progress in Champions League. The Express. 18 April 2019. Web.

clxii Thomas, Lyall. Ajax 2-3 Tottenham (Agg: 3-3): Lucas Moura hat-trick secures incredible Spurs win. Sky Sports. 9 May 2019. Web.

clxiii Liverpool FC. The Road to Madrid. Liverpool FC. June 2019. Web.

clxiv Ducker, James. Harry Kane: I'm still not over Champions League final defeat. The Telegraph. 19 July 2019. Web.

clxv Simpson, Christopher. Harry Kane Talks Champions League Final Defeat, Spurs Aiming for EPL Title. Bleacher Report. 10 July 2019. Web.

clxvi Garcia, Javier. 0-1: Real Madrid fail to reach Audi Cup final. Real Madrid. 30 July 2019. Web.

clxvii Auid Media Center. Tottenham Hotspur wins the 2019 Audi Cup. Audi. 31 July 2019. Web.

clxviii Bundesiga. Serge Gnabry scores four in blockbuster seven-goal Bayern Munich win over Tottenham Hotspur. Bundesliga. 1 October 2019. Web.

clxix Shread, Joe. Mauricio Pochettino sacked by Tottenham. Sky Sports. 21 November 2019. Web.

clxx Tennery, Amy. Harry Kane sends message to Mauricio Pochettino after former boss joins Chelsea. The Independent. 2 June 2023. Web.

clxxi Aarons, Ed. José Mourinho appointed Tottenham manager after Pochettino sacked. The Guardian. 20 November 2019. Web.

clxxii Jones, Gareth. West Ham 2-3 Tottenham: Jose Mourinho wins first game as Spurs boss. The Sporting Life. 23 November 2019. Web.

clxxiii Jurejko, Jonathan. Tottenham Hotspur 5-0 Burnley. BBC Sport. 7 December 2019. Web.

clxxiv Oscroft, Tim. Southampton 1-0 Tottenham Hotspur. BBC Sport. 1 January 2020. Web.

clxxv Premier League. How has the COVID-19 pandemic affected Premier League matches? Premier League. 15 June 2020. Web.

clxxvi Veal, Jonathan. Harry Kane on course to return for Tottenham when Premier League restarts after coronavirus postponement. The Independent. 24 March 2021. Web.

clxxvii Clayton, Freddie. Spurs finish sixth and qualify for Europa League after draw with Palace. Eurosport. 26 July 2020. Web.

clxxviii Brand, Gerard. Tottenham 0-1 Everton: Impressive Everton earn winning start in poor Spurs display. Sky Sports. 14 September 2020. Web.

clxxix Mendola, Nicholas. Spurs' Kane, Son rip through Southampton. NBC Sports. 20 September 2020. Web.

clxxx Tottenham Hotspur. Four-goal Sonny: "For me, Harry is Man of the Match!" Tottenham Hotspur. 21 September 2020. Web.

clxxxi Wilkinson, Jack. Manchester United 1-6 Tottenham: Spurs put shambolic 10-man United to the sword. Sky Sports. 5 October 2022. Web.

clxxxii Oscroft, Tim. Tottenham Hotspur 3-3 West Ham United. BBC Sport. 18 October 2020. Web.

clxxxiii Badshah, Nadeem. Premier League: Jose Mourinho's Tottenham Hotspur Go Top With Impressive Win Over Manchester City. Eurosport. 21 November 2011. Web.

clxxxiv Sky Sports. Ludogorets 1-3 Tottenham: Harry Kane scores 200th goal for Spurs in much-improved European showing. Sky Sports. 6 November 2020. Web.

clxxxv Marsh, Charlotte. Tottenham 1-1 Chelsea (5-4 pens): Spurs through to

Carabao Cup quarter-finals on penalties after late equaliser. Sky Sports. 30 September 2020. Web.

clxxxvi BeIN Sports. Carabao Cup final moved from February to April. BeIN. 21 December 2020. Web.

clxxxvii ESPN. Kane scores 250th goal, Tottenham beat Arsenal in north London derby. ESPN. 17 May 2023. Web.

clxxxviii Hynter, David. Harry Kane and Son Heung-min score as Tottenham beat Leeds to go third. The Guardian. 2 January 2021. Web.

clxxxix Steinberg, Jacob. 'Both ankles getting big': Mourinho says Kane could be out for 'a few weeks'. The Guardian. 29 January 2021. Web.

cxc George-Miller, Dustin. Wolfsberg 1-4 Tottenham: Spurs roll to comfortable Europa League win in Budapest. Cartilage Free Captain. 18 February 2021. Web.

cxci Reid, Andrew. 'Ridiculous': Football world stunned by 'unbelievable' Harry Kane act. Yahoo Sports Australia. 7 March 2021. Web.

cxcii Outlook. Tottenham 4-0 Wolfsberger (8-1 agg): Dele Alli Bicycle Kick Sends Spurs Into Europa League Last 16. Outlook India. 25 February 2021. Web.

cxciii Barlow, Matt. Tottenham 2-0 Dinamo Zagreb: Harry Kane double puts Spurs in control of Europa League last 16 tie as striker takes his goal tally to 26 for the season. The Daily Mail. 11 March 2021. Web.

cxciv Marsh, Charlotte. Dinamo Zagreb 3-0 Tottenham (agg 3-2): Spurs crash out of Europa League after Mislav Orsic hat-trick. Sky Sports. 19 March 2021. Web.

cxcv Olley, James. Jose Mourinho sacked as Tottenham manager. ESPN. 19 April 2021. Web.

cxcvi Keighley, Freddie. Harry Kane explains why Jose Mourinho "didn't work" at Tottenham. The Mirror. 21 May 2021. Web.

cxcvii Edwards, John. City Beat Spurs To Win Fourth Consecutive Carabao Cup. Manchester City. 25 April 2021. Web.

cxcviii Lake, Jefferson. Harry Kane: Tottenham striker wins Premier League Golden Boot award for third time. Sky Sports. 23 May 2021. Web.

cxcix Law, Matt. Harry Kane tells Tottenham he wants to leave club this summer. The Telegraph. 17 May 2021. Web.

cc Gilmour, Paul. Harry Kane to stay at Tottenham: Why striker has committed to Spurs and what the future may hold. Sky Sports. 26 August 2021. Web.

cci Kane, Harry. Tweet. Twitter. 25 August 2021. Web.

ccii Tula, Ishandeb. Nuno Espirito Santos is appointed as the new head coach of Tottenham Hotspur. The Sports News. 1 July 2021. Web.

cciii McNulty, Phil. Tottenham Hotspur 1-0 Manchester City. BBC Sport. 15 August 2021. Web.

cciv Husband, Ben. Tottenham 3-0 Pacos de Ferreira: 5 talking points as Harry Kane caps return with a brace. The Mirror. 26 August 2021. Web.

ccv Magowan, Alistair. Newcastle United 2-3 Tottenham Hotspur. BBC Sport. 17 October 2021. Web.

ccvi Sky Sports. Nuno Espirito Santo: Tottenham sack head coach. Sky Sports. 1 November 2021. Web.

ccvii Hynter, David. Antonio Conte talks up Tottenham ambitions after checking in as manager. The Guardian. 2 November 2021. Web.

ccviii Ruthven, Graham. Harry Kane Scores 20-Minute Hat-Trick As Tottenham Cruise To Victory Over Mura In Europa Conference League. Eurosport. 1 October 2021. Web.

ccix Jones, Mark. Furious Rennes refuse to recognise Tottenham postponement and insist match will go ahead. The Mirror. 8 December 2021. Web.

ccx Hynter, David. Spurs out of Europe after UEFA awards Rennes 3-0 win for cancelled game. The Guardian. 20 December 2021. Web.

ccxi BBC Sport. Wolverhampton Wanderers 2-2 Tottenham Hotspur. BBC. 22 September 2021. Web.

ccxii Chelsea FC. Spurs out of Europe after UEFA awards Rennes 3-0 win for cancelled game. Chelsea FC. 12 January 2022. Web.

ccxiii Verri, Matt. Tottenham 3-1 Brighton LIVE! Kane brace in win - FA Cup result, match stream and latest updates today. The Evening Standard. 5 February 2022. Web.

ccxiv Middlesbrough FC. Match Report: Boro 1 Tottenham Hotspur 0 (AET). Middlesbrough FC. 1 March 2022. Web.

ccxv ESPN. Harry Kane nets winner as Tottenham edge Man City in five-goal thriller. ESPN. 17 May 2023. Web.

ccxvi Black, Dan. RECAP: Burnley 1 Spurs 0. Burnley Express. 23 February 2022. Web.

ccxvii McNulty, Phil. Tottenham Hotspur 3-0 Arsenal. BBC Sport. 12 May 2022. Web.

ccxix Korea JoongAng Daily. Tottenham Hotspur put on a show with 6-3 win over Team K League. Korea JoongAng Daily. 13 July 2022. Web.

ccxx Grounds, Ben. Marseille 1-2 Tottenham: Pierre-Emile Hojbjerg secures dramatic comeback as Spurs reach Champions League last 16. Sky Sports. 2 November 2022. Web.

[ccxxi] Sky Sports. Tottenham 4-3 Leeds: Rodrigo Bentancur double rescues Spurs in pulsating encounter with Leeds. Sky. 12 November 2022. Web.

[ccxxii] Mackenzie, Alasdair. Harry Kane Becomes Tottenham's All-Time Top Scorer As 267th Goal Breaks Jimmy Greaves Record - 'Huge Moment For Me'. Eurosport. 5 February 2023. Web.

[ccxxiii] Begley, Emlyn. Leicester City 4-1 Tottenham Hotspur. BBC Sport. 11 February 2023. Web.

[ccxxiv] Richardson, David. Tottenham 0-0 AC Milan (agg 0-1): Antonio Conte's side dumped out of Champions League as 15-year trophy drought continues. Sky Sports. 9 March 2023. Web.

[ccxxv] Burton, Chris. Antonio Conte SACKED by Tottenham after savage rant at Daniel Levy & club's trophy record. GOAL. 26 March 2023. Web.

[ccxxvi] Newcastle United. Newcastle United 6 Tottenham Hotspur 1. Newcastle United. 23 April 2023. Web.

[ccxxvii] Rayner, Stuart. Leeds United 1 Tottenham Hotspur 4: All defiance gone as Whites limp out of Premier League without a whimper. Yorkshire Post. 28 May 2023. Web.

[ccxxviii] Sheen, Tom. Harry Kane: England debut goal was the best moment of my career. The Independent. 27 March 2015. Web.

[ccxxix] Shearer, Alan. Harry Kane's chance has come and gone at Euro 2016, Jamie Vardy and Daniel Sturridge must start up front. The Sun. 16 June 2016. Web.

[ccxxx] Samuel, Martin. England 1-2 Iceland: Three Lions suffer the ultimate humiliation by falling to embarrassing defeat against tournament minnows before Roy Hodgson resigns 20 minutes after final whistle. The Daily Mail. 27 June 2016. Web.

[ccxxxi] Fifield, Dominic. Gareth Southgate rewards Harry Kane with England captaincy against Scotland. The Guardian. 9 June 2017. Web.

[ccxxxii] Mokbel, Sami. Wayne Rooney set to lose England captain role as Gareth Southgate phases out permanent skipper. The Daily Mail. 16 March 2017. Web.

[ccxxxiii] The FA. Harry Kane To Captain England At 2018 World Cup. The FA. 22 May 2018. Web.

[ccxxxiv] McNulty, Phil. Tunisia 1-2 England. BBC Sport. 18 June 2018. Web.

[ccxxxv] Coleman, Joe. PRINCE HARRY 'We had fun' – England captain Harry Kane praises Three Lions after Panama rout and eyes Golden Boot after hat-trick heroics. Talk Sport. 24 June 2018. Web.

[ccxxxvi] Verschueren, Gianni. England Beat Colombia on Penalties, Advance to World Cup Quarter-Finals. The Bleacher Report. 3 July 2018. Web.

[ccxxxvii] West, Jenna. England's Harry Kane Wins World Cup Golden Boot

With Six Goals. Sports Illustrated. 15 July 2018. Web.

ccxxxviii Wilkinson, Jack. England 2-1 Croatia: Harry Kane scores dramatic late winner. Sky Sports. 19 November 2018. Web.

ccxxxix UEFA. Kosovo 0-4 England: Kane scores amid late goal glut. UEFA. 17 November 2019. Web.

ccxl Jones, Lewis. Ukraine 0-4 England: Three Lions book Euro 2020 semi-final at Wembley vs Denmark. Sky Sports. 4 July 2021. Web.

ccxli Rayner, Stuart. Harry Kane fires England to Euro 2020 final. Yorkshire Post. 7 July 2021. Web.

ccxlii Hynter, David. Italy crush England's dreams after winning Euro 2020 on penalties. The Guardian. 11 July 2021. Web.

ccxliii Ouzia, Malik. San Marino 0-10 England: Harry Kane scores four as Three Lions book World Cup spot with rout. The Evening Standard. 15 November 2021. Web.

ccxliv Smith, Frank. Harry Kane's England hat-tricks. England Football. 12 November 2021. Web.

ccxlv Humayun, Ali. What does Nations League relegation mean for England? The Athletic. 23 September 2022. Web.

ccxlvi Burt, Jason. Under-fire Gareth Southgate battles short memories ahead of loaded Germany match. The Telegraph. 25 September 2022. Web.

ccxlvii Reid, James. England 6-2 Iran - FIFA World Cup Qatar 2022 match centre. England Football. 21 November 2022. Web.

ccxlviii McNulty, Phil. England 0-0 USA. BBC Sport. 25 November 2022. Web.

ccxlix Smith, Peter. World Cup 2022 - Wales 0-3 England: Marcus Rashford and Phil Foden star to set up Senegal last-16 clash and knock out Rob Page's side. Sky Sports. 29 November 2022. Web.

ccl Barton, Aaron. England 3-0 Senegal: Harry Kane Scores As Three Lions Secure Last-16 Win To Set Up France Showdown In Quarter-Finals. Eurosport. 5 December 2022. Web.

ccli Walker, Ron. Harry Kane's penalty miss: The factors behind England captain's failure from the spot against France at World Cup. Sky Sports. 14 December 2022. Web.

cclii Hynter, David. Harry Kane admits World Cup penalty miss will haunt him for rest of his life. The Guardian. 5 January 2023. Web.

ccliii Smith, Rory. We Know Nothing About Harry Kane. The New York Times. 11 June 2021. Web.

ccliv Packer, Amy. Harry Kane. Life As I Know It. Life Beyond Sport. 2019. Web.

cclv Wilson, Ben. Harry Kane reveals his secret to staying chilled at the World

Cup: playing Fortnite. Games Rader. 3 July 2018. Web.

[cclvi] Ursy, Rob. What role will Harry Kane play in FIFA 17's The Journey? Cartilage Free Captain. 13 September 2016. Web.

[cclvii] Brown, Kevin. EXCLUSIVE: England captain Harry Kane on golf, Tiger, Augusta and the World Cup. Today's Golfer. 18 November 2022. Web.

[cclviii] Brown, Georgia. Harry Kane's family: Who are the England captain's wife and children? Hello Magazine. 19 February 2023. Web.

[cclix] Shahid, Sharnaz. Harry Kane comforts heartbroken wife Katie after she bursts into tears over England's Euro loss. Hello Magazine. 17 July 2021. Web.

[cclx] Sky Sports. Harry Kane Foundation launched on World Mental Health Day with aim of tackling mental health stigma. Sky Sports. 10 October 2022. Web.

[cclxi] Summerscales, Rob. Harry Kane Hits 30-Goal Mark For Second Time In Premier League Career. Fan Nation. 28 May 2023. Web.

[cclxii] Potts, Michael. This is the date Harry Kane will beat Alan Shearer's Premier League goal record. The Radio Times. 6 February 2023. Web.

Printed in Great Britain
by Amazon

53318325R00057